Dec 17

per Kusheena

(per Becky)

ENDORSEMENTS

"Over the years I've come to treasure Bob Hamp's remarkable ability to help us all look at familiar things in new, transforming ways. His latest book is no exception. I wholeheartedly recommend Think Differently Lead Differently to any person with a heart for having a positive, eternal impact on the people around them."

Kari Jobe
Dove award-winning Artist

"Long before I began reading Bob Hamp's books I listened to him teach. From the first time I heard him I was fascinated at the fresh revelation he had and the unique way he has of presenting truth. That is what I found in this book. It is fresh revelation presented in a clear and compelling manner. As a pastor and church leader for over thirty years I was engaged, encouraged and challenged beginning with the first page. This book is a must read for leaders in all positions and on all levels."

Jimmy Evans
Founder & CEO of MarriageToday

"This is one of the most impactful books I have ever read on leadership! Bob Hamp has a simple yet profound way of communicating how we must learn to think differently in order to lead differently. And we can't think differently unless we are connected to the Person of Christ, allowing Him to truly transform us on the inside. We must engage the Voice of the Spirit and the heart of Christ, not just the letter of the law, so that we can think and see the way God does. In this book, Bob reminds us that depending on and being connected to God is the only way to avoid the trap of self-sufficiency. This is a great book for leaders, but a must read for everyone!"

Nancy Alcorn
Founder and President of Mercy Ministries International

"I am fascinated by Bob's insight into spiritual leadership. This book is a must read for anyone who wishes to influence others with health and integrity. Bob is a trusted voice in the local church and into the lives of those leading our congregations."

Brady Boyd
New Life Church, Colorado Springs
Author of Sons and Daughters, and Let Her Lead

"Every pastor and ministry leader needs to read this book! Thought-provoking and motivating, Think Differently Lead Differently challenges leaders to inspire the body of Christ to be a part of something bigger than ourselves by igniting a movement of leading people to not just hear ABOUT God, but to have a life changing Encounter WITH God.   If you want to experience a radical transformation in your community, you will love this book."

Amy Ford
Co-Founder and President of Embrace Grace
Author of A Bump in Life: True Stories of Hope
& Courage during an Unplanned Pregnancy

"In his new book, Think Differently Lead Differently, Bob Hamp brings his keen insight and unique approach to the issue of healthy leadership. More than offering tweaks to the status quo of organizational management, he offers a deeply biblical and perhaps even a culturally subversive view into what it truly means to provide leadership within the family of God. It's no good to lead into change if we're changing the wrong things. This book is revolutionary in the way it addresses Jesus' kingdom message, his intentions for the church, and the implications that follow for leading in alignment with Jesus' way of seeing reality. Every leader needs to read this book. I hope many will."

Alan Smith
Senior Pastor, Catch The Fire DFW
Author of Unveiled: The Transforming Power of God's Presence and Voice

THINK DIFFER ENTLY LEAD DIFFER ENTLY

Bringing reformation in your heart,
your home and your organization

A book by
BOB HAMP

ISBN: 978-0-9914820-5-4
Library of Congress Control Number: 2014939226

Visit www.bobhamp.com for additional ministry information.

Cover & Layout Design by Scott Cornelius and ThinkTree Media

Printed in the USA

CONTENTS

ACKNOWLEDGMENTS

Never have the truths I write about seemed more real to me than in the process of getting this crazy book written. It has been two years from the time of conception to birth, but more importantly, it has been two years filled with rich connections and friendships, making the journey not only bearable, but wonderful. I would like to take a moment to express my thanks.

As with my first book, I am deeply aware that others have significantly taught and influenced me. Specifically Bill Johnson's teaching series, Leading from the Heart, which gave me great hope for the kind of leadership I write about here.

Certainly, I'm grateful to my family, all of whom know me and see me in different ways and have dreamed with me and for me as this project moved from crazy ideas to words on pages. My mother-in-law, Jettie Omdahl again did double duty as both supportive family and editorial expertise.

I am grateful to my Pastor, Robert Morris and the elders at Gateway Church who have both shown me how and allowed me latitude to grow as a spiritual leader. I am particularly deeply indebted to David Holland who is far more than a great writer and editor. He rescued me from the mess of a manuscript and came alongside me with both vision and clarity to turn the muddy waters of my manuscript into the best wine of the night. He also became a great friend.

Similarly I owe a huge thanks to Brandon Day of ThinkTree Media for helping me navigate the waters of taking my piles of ideas and turning them into a beautiful, palatable product. He also is a great friend.

The friendship of Alan and Nancy Smith, Jimmy James, Kerrie Oles, Peggy Stevens and dozens of people who called me, e-mailed me, texted me and hunted me down out of the blue in order to tell me they were praying for me has been a deeply necessary well of support and strength in what has proven to be the most difficult years of my life. Thanks to each of you for holding up my arms and my heart while I wrestled this one into existence.

INTRODUCTION

AN INVITATION TO LEAD DIFFERENTLY

Look with me through a window of time and space to a semi-fictional moment in ancient history. The leader of a fledgling nation is preparing to move in and take new territory. Just the other side of the border is the first of many walled cities. This leader sends his two top generals in to spy out the land and develop the campaign to begin their conquest.

The first general comes back with a positive report, and makes his presentation to the monarch.

"I have carefully checked the terrain and the next six months weather," he begins. "After consulting with the neighboring military forces, and looking back through the journals of ancient history, I have good news."

"Proceed," says his king.

"If we launch our campaign in the next week, which should give me plenty of time to brief our men and shore up our supplies, I believe that a six month siege will significantly weaken their war machine as well as their wills. With minimal cost and very little loss of life to our own people, I think we can take this city in about half a year."

He stands back, pleased with his plan and the manner in which he had delivered it. Expecting a fond response from their monarch and a similar report from his colleague, he waits to hear the second report.

"And you?" the King queries, turning to the second general.

The second leader steps forward with a gleam in his eye and a tenuous posture. "Well, your majesty," he begins. "I don't know any other way to tell you this, but I believe that if we enter the land tomorrow and march around the city every day for the next week, on the last day we can all shout and blow our trumpets, and the city walls will fall down, allowing us to take possession of the city by the end of the week."

What kind of leader would make this preposterous kind of recommendation in the face of the collective wisdom of history, tacticians, and years of siege-warfare? This is precisely the right question to ask and precisely the question this book will seek to answer. The kind of leader that would make such an outlandish suggestion is a spiritual leader.

More specifically, the kind of leader that would make such a suggestion is a leader who is keenly aware that while he must wage his campaigns on the platform of visible reality, he is entirely surrounded by and interactive with another reality, an invisible realm which operates on a different set of rules and principles. Only a leader who acknowledges the existence of such a realm and knows the ins and outs of it would dare to make such a recommendation.

A spiritual leader would be willing to reexamine the presuppositions of years of military experts and tacticians. A spiritual leader, thinking rightly, and aware of all pertinent factors would be able to recognize when human wisdom is sufficient and when and how the experts are limited by their own perspective. A spiritual leader like this would be willing to Think Differently before he ever recommends or implements a single strategy.

This book is written for men and women who are, or wish to be, spiritual leaders. Because this is the target, the first half of the book is largely devoted to reexamining some key presuppositions, followed by several chapters of overt discussion of the territory and targets of spiritual leadership.

Before recommending any of the targets and tactics in the second half of the book, I want to be sure we are thinking rightly about the big picture.

*****

Imagine with me for a moment that we take the greatest leadership tools and teachers available and deliver them to a colony of lemmings in northern Canada. You know, lemmings, the cute furry creatures that are believed to follow each other en masse off the edge of arctic cliffs.

Now let's say we give them the ten most valuable leadership lessons known to man and turn them loose. Have we done them a favor? Or have we in fact possibly harmed them? I would submit that unless we first teach them the difference between a cliff and solid ground, great leadership principles might hasten their early departure from the planet.

Let's not take this illustration too far, as I do not believe that we are all running headlong off a cliff, but the principle remains; before we teach good leadership we must first clearly understand the territory and targets in which such leadership must take place.

As the first half comes to a close, with a reexamination of some crucial assumptions, we will turn our attention to the targets, strategies and goals of a spiritual leader. In other words, once we consider ways to Think Differently, we will turn our attention to ways to Lead Differently.

Stay with me. A journey like this can challenge not only assumptions but can sometimes challenge your own personal comfort. But if you will stay through to the end, I believe you will not only regain your footing but you will find yourself with new direction, new ways of seeing, and a new perspective on leading in this thing called the Kingdom of God.

*****

In the chapters that follow I hope to take you on a journey of discovery—or perhaps I should say re-discovery—because I believe we long ago lost something vital and wonderful. This journey will require an open mind and receptive heart because I'm probably going to challenge a few of your long-held assumptions about our roles as leaders and shepherds of God's people. Be warned! Pre-suppositions will be examined. Dusty, rusty, calcified paradigms may break loose and shift. A few sacred cows may even be gored.

Along the way we must ask what it was that Jesus actually came to Earth to do—and find a potentially surprising answer. We will explore the *why* of the Gospel, but before we talk about the why we will have to take some time to talk about the *what*. You see, Jesus had in mind some very specific objectives for His brief time on Earth. And because He had those objectives, He also had in mind some specific strategies for achieving them.

> "BEFORE WE TEACH GOOD LEADERSHIP WE MUST FIRST CLEARLY UNDERSTAND THE TERRITORY AND TARGETS IN WHICH SUCH LEADERSHIP MUST TAKE PLACE."

We will take an approach to the Gospels that assumes nothing in them is random—that nothing Jesus said or did was accidental or incidental. We'll assume that when Jesus spoke, He did not chase a single rabbit trail in the way you and I are prone to do. We'll take Him at His word that He only spoke the things He heard (with His spiritual ears) His Father speaking, and that He only did those things He saw (with His spiritual eyes) the Father doing.

We will note that on numerous occasions when Jesus was presented with a question, He seemed to ignore the question He was asked, answering an utterly different one. Was He being dense? Of course not. Confused? No. It's just that people then, like you and I now, tend to ask the wrong question because we operate from flawed assumptions or suffer from various forms of tunnel vision.

Nicodemus came to Jesus under cover of darkness wanting to discuss Jesus' credentials: *"Rabbi, we know that You are a teacher come from God; for no one can do these signs that You do unless God is with him"* (John 3:2). Jesus completely ignored the proposed topic and "answered" with a statement about Nicodemus' own spiritual condition: *"Jesus answered and said to him, 'Most assuredly, I say to you, unless one is born again, he cannot see the kingdom of God'"* (3:3). Nicodemus, like most of us, was operating under a faulty paradigm and as a result—with sound logic and the best of intentions—he came to the right person and asked the wrong question. It's a very human tendency with a long, distinguished history.

> **"WE CAN ONLY LEAD PEOPLE WELL IF WE'RE CLEAR AND ACCURATE ABOUT WHERE WE'RE LEADING THEM."**

Study Jesus' interactions with questioners and you find that He frequently appears to go off course with His answers. As in the case of Nicodemus, the problem isn't with Jesus' answers; it's with the mindset of the questioner. Even when Jesus appears to go off course, He is actually right on target—refusing to waste time and pressing directly into the real heart of the matter.

Jesus spent a significant portion of His teaching ministry simply trying to jar His listeners out of their old, flawed ways of viewing the world. He stood in front of a throng on a Galilean hillside and declared (paraphrasing):

> "You have heard it said, 'Don't murder.' But I say to you don't even hate, because if you hate, you've already killed your brother. You've heard it said, 'Don't commit adultery.' But I say to you don't even look on a woman with lust, because if you have lust inside your heart, you've already committed adultery inside your heart." (Insert the Jimmy Carter joke of your choice here.)

So Jesus begins the most revolutionary sermon ever delivered to human ears with the assertion that His hearers are thinking wrongly about some things. At the heart of His early preaching—as well as that of forerunner John the Baptist's—was this simple message: *"Repent, for the kingdom of God is near."* Like most other things, we have some deeply held presuppositions about the meaning of the word repent. But a faithful rendering of the Greek word translated "repent" in the New Testament is simply "think in a whole new way." Not just think a new thing. Not just add some new information content to your mind. But completely change the process. In other words, "Think differently." (That would make a wonderful title for a book or two!)

A few years ago my book *Think Differently Live Differently* laid out a revolutionary approach to personal transformation and living in all the freedom Jesus died to purchase for us. In the years since its publication, I've heard from thousands of people, many of them pastors and church leaders, who have kindly let me know what a profound impact that book had on their life and ministry. In great humility and genuine astonishment, I can tell you that each month I receive many more invitations to come speak on those truths than I can possibly accept.

The book you now hold in your hands is the logical extension of that first work. If individuals were and are in need of a more authentically biblical way of engaging the subjects of freedom, identity and purpose, how much more are we as Christian leaders and shepherds desperate for a new such model? We can only lead people well if we're clear and accurate about where we're leading them.

Think Differently Lead Differently is my humble offering in the cause of addressing this need. On the pages that follow, the relevance and aptness of the parable of "The Game" that begins on the next page and reappears throughout the book will come increasingly into focus. And yes, I may challenge some long-held and largely unexamined assumptions about our roles as leaders, disciple-ers, mentors, coaches, and pastors.

Stay with me. Stay open. It's going to be fun.

A PARABLE—
PART I

They couldn't ignore him this week. He was going to drive a motorcycle on the stage, right when they least expected it. His team was working on the mechanics of this, and had promised him that it was possible.

The guy down the street was midway through the newest series from headquarters, and had told him how great it was. All the banners and videos supported a power packed exposé of the Original Copy. The Old Rules had never seemed so fresh, his friend told him.

But his people needed something to wake them up. All the promise of deeply changed lives and excited crowds now seemed to be yet another instance of minor impact and disappointing results.

Oh, his people said nice things, but they always said nice things. They were nice people. At least he was pretty sure they were.

This week, the Old Book would seem big, and powerful. Like the roar of a Harley Davidson. But inwardly he felt the pressure. What would he do the next week? Could he really keep their attention? Worse, was he really changing their lives like he promised? Their lives—what about his own?

The last several years seemed a constant string of trying to figure out what would really be the key to the breakthrough that he felt was always just out of reach. Something about this constant struggle continued to nag at the back of his mind. Surely this was not the way this was supposed to work. He pushed the nagging feeling down again and turned to his tech team.

If this didn't work, he would try something else. He was after all, a Master Teacher of The Game.

CHAPTER 1

CHANGE THE RIGHT THING

"Meet the new boss ... the same as the old boss."
—The Who, Won't Get Fooled Again

We can't solve problems by using the same kind of thinking we used when we created them."
—Albert Einstein

I experienced an unexpected flash of understanding as I drove past my son's high school campus one day. He was on the basketball team at the time and as I passed his school I recall thinking, *Isn't it interesting that the basketball team never meets in a classroom. They always meet in the gym.* In other words, they don't try to develop basketball players by teaching them theoretically about the game of basketball. They develop them by engaging them experientially, vigorously, joyously in the game of basketball.

In that moment I received a flood of insight about the way we as church leaders have generally gone about our mission of developing Jesus followers. Like a rolling explosion inside my brain the parable about "The Game" began to unfold as an allegory for the way we have historically done "church" and "discipleship."

It resonated strongly in part because I consistently find myself pondering questions like: Are we as leaders being effective in changing lives? Are we discipling people the way Jesus would have expected us to disciple them?

Are we doing what Jesus did? As I drove past the school I realized that *this is precisely what we do!* We put people in classrooms or auditoriums and try to teach them about something that can only be experienced. We give them a knowing instead of a *living*. Theory, not practice. We can obsessively involve them in rule following or style issues or theories of proper Jesus-following without ever actually involving them in, you know, the actual following of Jesus.

MISDIAGNOSE—MISTREAT

It's the middle of the 14th Century and the Black Plague is laying waste to Europe. The pandemic is killing people faster than the living can bury them. In many cities more than 50% of the population has been lost. Maddeningly, no one seems to have a clue about what causes it.

A few observant leaders, however, have noticed a pattern. Wherever the plague is most severe, there seem to be a lot of cats hanging around. And come to think of it, in places with very few cats, the plague is rarely present. Furthermore, have you ever noticed how indifferent and stealthy cats are? They're obviously hiding something and up to no good.

The evidence is persuasive. A conclusion is reached: *Cats are obviously causing the plague.* In city after city cats are exterminated by the thousands. And in those cities, without exception, the spread of the plague accelerates.

What these enterprising, well-intentioned leaders don't know is that the pathogen responsible for the Black Death is the *Yersinia pestis* bacterium, which was carried by a type of flea that was perfectly adapted to live on rats. It is flea-infested rats carrying this horrific scourge from city to city. And feral cats are drawn by the presence of the rats and are working to keep the rat population at bay.

That's right. Europe's leaders destroyed the only thing standing between them and the plague. They changed the wrong thing.

Every day well-meaning leaders in the Church do something very similar and for similar reasons—that is, they're trying to help people. They see a problem and they want to solve it. They see pain and want to heal it. They see dysfunction and want to correct it. But all too often, they change the wrong thing. Their passionately written and administered "prescription" doesn't cure the ill. Indeed, the "remedy" often makes the ailment worse.

As Bethel's Bill Johnson likes to say, "We will always mistreat what we misdiagnose."

I recall coming across a blog post by a pastor a few years ago that exemplifies

9

this syndrome. The author had just watched a pastor friend suffer disgrace after being caught in a highly public moral failure, leaving yet another black mark against the reputation of the cause he loved and served. It was clearly more than he could bear.

His friend had fallen and the words he poured into that heartfelt, agonized blog post made it clear that he cared desperately. With the passion of a man who has reached his limit and is compelled to act, he turned to the Church and delivered a written plea. "We must change, we must find the answer to this ill that plagues our leaders," he cried. With all the right motives and a yearning driven by grief and frustration he offered his prescription. And with well-intentioned fervor, the writer called for more of the same medicine that had failed his friend.

He recommended changing the wrong thing.

In times of crisis or rapid change both individuals and organizations tend to cry out for change. Movements do as well. They champion their preferred answer to the current crisis. Much like the cat-killers of plague-ravaged Europe, their chosen solution is a direct reflection of their understanding of the problem. And with remarkable consistency, that understanding is flawed. Mis-diagnosis leads to mis-treatment.

Nevertheless, church leaders do their best to pioneer a new and better path. Sadly, the reasons, motivations and methods of change often only set up a new version of the old system. It *feels* new, because it's cosmetically different. But too often time reveals that the "new" approach is simply a fresh wrapper on an old system. Just as frequently, sweeping systemic change does happen—but sooner or later the well-intentioned authors of the change discover they changed the wrong thing.

For many reasons the Church is particularly prone to changing the wrong thing. The surrounding circumstances shift. Leaders respond by pushing specific agendas of change. Eventually the flux becomes a new homeostatic balance—a new normal. Then the surrounding circumstances shift ...

Lather. Rinse. Repeat.

By way of example, let's look with fresh eyes at a time in church history when major change happened and ask ourselves if our forefathers indeed changed the right thing. I'm referring to the birth of the Reformation. I think that qualifies as a pivotal point, don't you?

Martin Luther reads the book of Romans at a time in which the church is in a state of absolute humanism and greed. Among other offenses, the Church is selling "indulgences"—man-made systematized corruption whereby people are told they can purchase justification in God's eyes from the Church. As

Luther travels the Romans road, the Spirit of God moves on his heart. God enlightens his mind to a transformational truth. He weeps at the power and beauty of the revelation. Justification, the salvation of the human soul, comes by faith alone. He is profoundly moved and leaves this encounter with the voice of God with a new mission—to proclaim this revelation to others.

His proclamation and the movement it sparked is known as the Reformation. As you probably know, it represented a massive shift in the way millions relate to God as people discovered they could receive the free gift of God by faith alone. As a result, the flailing Church establishment lost a great deal of its grip on the minds of those people. Change happened. Significant change. The Church and therefore the world took a major turn, and History has moved from that point forward on a different trajectory. It is almost universally assumed in the Protestant/Evangelical world that Luther changed the right thing.

But what if he didn't?

Picture with me a slightly different scenario. What if instead of proclaiming to the world the content of his personal revelation, Martin Luther had also proclaimed the process by which this truth arrived? What if instead of "justification by faith alone," Martin Luther began to proclaim this: "God speaks to people personally"?

In reality, Luther proclaimed the *content* of his encounter to the world and completely ignored the *process* by which he arrived at that content.

> **"THE REASONS, MOTIVATIONS AND METHODS OF CHANGE OFTEN ONLY SET UP A NEW VERSION OF THE OLD SYSTEM."**

This is why we are so prone to changing the wrong thing. We are content-focused rather than process-focused, so we tend to try to "fix" outcomes rather than fixing the process that repeatedly, faithfully produces those outcomes. Thus, fluid moves of God quickly calcify into brittle law when we fallible humans deliver the content of the move and fail to communicate the process. When God speaks, we deliver His words instead of the transformative, revolutionary key—hearing His voice.

Content is today's "manna," to use the Israelites' miraculous wilderness experience as a metaphor. What God said to you today is what He said to you today. It's content. But the wonderful reality that God provides manna every single day is a process. And if we try to hang onto yesterday's content instead of the process as a whole, we end up with a jar of rotten food.

This is precisely what happens when we try to solve problems—at a personal level and at the corporate level of the Church—when things around us are in flux. We look at the content and say, "Hey, we've done it this way for a long time but it's no longer working. What if instead of doing it that way we do it *this* way?" In doing so we're essentially saying, "Let's throw out this old content and get new content. Maybe that will work." The question is, where does this tendency come from?

The third chapter of Galatians actually describes how this happens. Here, Paul addresses the Galatians who are beginning to be bogged down by this mysterious thing known as law. He begins the chapter describing the wonderful way in which the Galatians experienced the beginnings of their faith journey. They heard and believed, and in so doing they received the Spirit. He then chides them for what happens next. "Having begun in the Spirit, do you now try to perfect yourselves by the flesh?" he asks.

It is a frustratingly predictable progression. God tells us something. Then invariably we turn God's declaration of a "will be" into an "ought to." His promise becomes an obligation. Through some sort of perverse alchemy we transform hope into hardship.

What if, instead, when God told us something, we begin to realize that in the act of speaking He has connected us to the very power that will achieve what He has said?

Law is anything that provokes us to self-effort. Even yesterday's revelation can become today's law. Bill Johnson likes to remind us that faith comes by hearing, not by having heard. God is both the Author and the Perfecter of our faith, and as such, He does not need us to loan Him our strength.

How something happens matters to God more than what happens. When He tells us, *"Not by might or power but by My Spirit"* (Zechariah 4:6), He is not just telling us that He will do something. He is also warning us how *not* to do it. He is warning us not to try it by our might or power. He is telling us about process.

We are in a state of unprecedented shift. The world around us, and every human system within it is shaking. Economies and governments alike, and even the natural, physical world is shaking and in many cases crumbling. The Church is no exception. Mainline denominations and large institutions are hemorrhaging people en masse. Simultaneously new churches are popping up and dotting the religious horizon. Some of this represents a shift in where "churched" people are attending. Some of this is a departure of people from the church. And some represents a new wave of unchurched people arriving at our doorsteps. What is undeniable is that change is happening, and we are all trying to grab the reins. We are all striving to understand these changes, and in some cases, actually drive the change.

Today we have a fresh opportunity to change the right thing. To do this, and to lead well in this season of shift, I'm convinced it is vital that we look through a particular set of lenses at the historic role of the Church and at God's unfolding plan. These lenses will focus on more than content. They will allow us to recognize and shape processes as well. Allow me to explain.

"YOU HAVE HEARD IT SAID"

I briefly referenced Jesus' first sermon—the Sermon on the Mount—in the Introduction. As I suggested there, this history-shaking discourse contains an entire section in which He addresses this type of change. He speaks to the crowd and at one point He reaches an almost rhythmic cadence.

"You have heard it said ..." He cries, "but I say to you ..." He repeats this compare-and-contrast pattern several times, announcing an invitation to think differently. He fills in the blank again and again, and viewed through the wrong set of lenses it can seem as if Jesus is delivering new and more challenging *content*. For example, He said: "You have heard it said do not murder, but I say to you do not hate." The content, or the specific rule just got harder, right? He raised the bar that we're required to jump over.

Or did He? Listen again to the pattern that Jesus establishes and repeats.

"You have heard (the content of the law), do not murder, but I say to you do not (have the kind of heart that processes people through your own pain and judgments), do not hate."

In other words, Jesus compares and contrasts the content of the law with the *processes* of our hearts. Put yet another way, "You have heard this content-centric rule, but I say to you do not have a heart that operates in this way." Jesus is pushing us not to merely replace old content with better, more effective content. Jesus is urging us to move away from content-centered thinking and toward process-centered thinking. He is urging us to move away from the noun of the Law to the verb of our hearts' movements. He is urging us to change the right thing. He is urging us to change the process, not the content. He came to show us a new *Way*, not a new *what*. (You may be aware that the movement we now call Christianity was originally referred to as "The Way." That's not an insignificant factoid.)

Content thinking and teaching is tempting because it is easier to understand, and it is easier to replicate. If it is easier to replicate, it is easier to multiply. This is a draw to us as church leaders because we all see the scope of the need. The breadth and depth of the condition of our world and the human population could easily overwhelm us as we begin to see it more clearly. The need to do more can lead to a temptation to focus on the more easily communicated and replicated content areas, instead of the transformational arenas of process.

If God is doing something effective, the temptation is to write it down and then distribute it as widely as possible. Codify, systematize, and multiply. Logical thinking tells us that this approach should multiply God's effectiveness. But again, more often than not, the books and curriculums that we develop are all designed to deliver content (systems, methodologies, rules, etc.). When we do this, people invariably take the new content and apply it to the same process they have always utilized. The old law is replaced by the new law, even though the problem has been law-ish thinking. New information will simply come in through the old process, and change may happen, but they will have changed the wrong thing. Again.

Henry Blackaby gives a fantastic illustration of this in his study, *Experiencing God.* He tells the story of a pastor who hears God tell him to start a bus ministry. As he follows God's direction, the church, of course, explodes with growth. As he grows in visibility, people begin to ask him the secret of his success.

"CONTENT THINKING AND TEACHING IS TEMPTING BECAUSE IT IS EASIER TO UNDERSTAND, AND IT IS EASIER TO REPLICATE."

Before too long, he begins to find ways to let others in on his secret to church growth. Faithfully transmitting his content, he speaks at conferences and writes books on how to grow your church through bus ministry. Other leaders latch onto the newest fad, and they all try to grow their churches based on one man's content. Of course, the real secret to his church growth was not bus ministry; it was hearing God and following His voice. The real key to church life and health was not his content, but rather the process that gave him access to that content. But that never got communicated.

When a generation or an era begins to shift, the danger is always that we simply deliver new content into the age-old processes. New ideas quickly lose their distinctive shape when tossed into the vat of an unchanged thought process. If the church is filled with a way of thinking that defines God as angry and demanding, every new discipleship strategy will be aimed at satisfying the wrath of an angry God. If Christianity has been tinged with humanism, new ideas will be seen as one more set of expectations to which we apply our human capabilities. Our way of thinking is like the lenses through which we view and process every new wind.

Every new idea, no matter how fresh and even revelatory, soaked in the marinade of law, becomes lifeless.

CHAPTER 2

HERE WE GO AGAIN

"It used to be about trying to do something. Now it's about trying to be someone."
—Margaret Thatcher, The Iron Lady

"Anyone who thinks sitting in church can make you a Christian must also think that sitting in a garage can make you a car."
—Garrison Keillor

Today we are poised at the edge again. We have one more opportunity to see massive change in our global church culture. How will we handle that opportunity? Like the man who wrote the impassioned plea to the church world on behalf of his fallen friend, will we give the same old prescription with just a bit more emotion behind it?

His prescription? It is the same prescription that has been offered to each generation. It can be summed up in two words: "Try harder." We dress it up a bit, but it is the same message simply repeated and amplified.

Read and memorize scripture. Be faithful to our quiet times. Have an accountability partner. And above all maintain your integrity. Those things sound great right? And certainly they are not wrong. The insidious thing about content-level change is that it is not "wrong." And because it is not wrong it can produce a false sense of security. "Not wrong" does not always equal right.

A meaningful difference must be conveyed between the content answer and a process answer. The above ideas must be more than just *what* to do. We must help people know *how* to do these things. And by how, I do not mean provide step-by-step instructions. I am specifically referring to the *way* in which these steps are carried out.

Let's borrow a formula from the master Teacher, Jesus Himself, to see if I can communicate the difference.

1. **You have heard it said** memorize more scripture **but I say to you** learn to let the living and active Word of God renew your mind. The first implies that if *you* somehow exert more memory power and retain more scriptural data you will be able to act differently. This actually seemed to backfire for the Pharisees, who had their entire Bible memorized yet were the principal opponent of the abundant life God sent Jesus to offer us.

   Renewing our minds does not mean replacing wrong data with right data, the knowledge of evil with the knowledge of good. Paul tells us that the problem with law is that it does not have the power to transform us. Memorizing scripture *alone* can simply become lifeless law and rigid rule keeping—leaving the work of transformation reliant on human capabilities, and therefore bound by human limitations.

   When God speaks He is creating. We can engage the V*oice,* not just the letter. We can move beyond merely learning the data of scripture, to learning *to think and see* like the Author. Let the words on the pages connect you to the Person of the Kingdom. Allow Him to point out core lies—deception in the deep places of your heart. Let Him show you false beliefs about Him and false beliefs about you, and about what's really *real.* More importantly, allow Him to tell you *truth,* because even identifying lies is not sufficient to change our behavior without the corresponding truth coming in to replace those lies.

2. **You have heard it said** have more consistent time alone with God **but I say to you** when you are alone with Him practice internal surrender. *What happens* during your time with God matters more than *how much* time you spend. In Luke 18:9-14, Jesus compared two guys, both of whom were praying. One told God how glad he was that he was not a bad guy and shared his moral resume. Certain that God was impressed, he prayed and spent time with God. The

other stood before God, and transparently professed his lack of qualification. He unashamedly told God he deserved nothing, and knew that his spiritual resume was a declaration of his need for help.

Both were spending time with God. It seemed that Jesus was more concerned with *the way* these men prayed than the mere fact that they were praying. Again, not the steps they went through, but the process of their hearts seemed to be the target of Jesus' teaching.

Jesus came to set the captives free, not to apprise us of His moral preferences. The restoration of our hearts, not the disciplining of our flesh, will transform our outward experience. Let Him heal the wounds of our lives; let Him exchange our heart of stone for His heart of flesh. Let Him do His work, instead of telling Him how well we have done ours.

To simply give people the instruction to pray more might fill our rooftops with men and women displaying their spiritual resumes.

3. **You have heard it said** practice accountability **but I say to you** the Holy Spirit comes to convict us of sin and righteousness and judgment; *so let Him do His job in you.* While it is true that Jesus tells us that in God's economy the opposite of evil is *truth* not *good* (John 3:20-21), truth sometimes eludes us in our limited sight. Even when we are trying to be ruthlessly accountable we cannot confess to another the things hidden deeply in our hearts that we ourselves have yet to see.

> **"JESUS CAME TO SET THE CAPTIVES FREE, NOT TO APPRISE US OF HIS MORAL PREFERENCES."**

Simply being able to tell another when we mess up is not sufficient to stop us from messing up. And even if it prevents us from behaving badly, it is unlikely to transform the content and processes of our hearts. Fear or respect of another's probing eyes may hold the beast at bay, but it does not have the power to crucify it. When the Holy Spirit brings light to the darkness in us and shows us that this darkness is no longer compatible with our new nature, the darkness is put to death, and the Holy Spirit ignites the righteousness of Christ in us.

4. **You have heard it said** maintain your integrity **but I say to you** learn how to take dominion and practice your authority as a son or daughter of the Living God. Somehow in our recommendations to one another we leave out one of the most significant aspects of Jesus' framework of thought. He clearly recognized and engaged a whole realm of reality that I will call "the invisible world." This is part of the creation that Adam was tasked with taking dominion over. This is still our assignment to this day.

I remind us again that Jesus came to set captives free. If a man or woman is under the influence of another kingdom and has no idea what Jesus has done to grant us authority in this life and how to practice this authority, we remain under the influence.

In Jesus' teachings in the Sermon on the Mount, He was not discarding the first part of the "you have heard it said" statements, He was trying to reveal the hidden traps behind the statements. I am in no way suggesting that we throw out Bible study, time with God, accountability, and integrity. I am, however *strongly* urging us to grow in awareness that salvation and freedom are the acts of God in our lives, not the result of arm-wrestling behavior, thoughts, and emotions into submission.

Behavior management has never been the objective. Transformation of the inner man and the restoration of God's created design in our souls is the objective. To offer the four solutions mentioned above as if they are sufficient for living the life we are called to is like urging a man to swing on a trapeze, telling him the nets below are there in case he falls, but neglecting to tell him that the nets are not anchored to their support and, therefore, will not hold his weight.

God did not send His Son to command us to behave like someone we are not. He sent Him to restore our factory settings so we might behave and think and feel like who He is in us.

CHANGE THE "HOW" NOT THE "WHAT"

The above illustrations were designed to illustrate how the "what" of Christian counsel can be insufficient, and in some cases, even contrary to what God actually has in mind. Indeed, the goal of this book can largely be summed up in this idea: leading God's Church is often much more about the "how" than it is about the "what." It can seem counterintuitive—perhaps even a little heretical—to the mind that has been raised on "do," "don't," and "try harder." But the truth is, if we get the "how" right, it actually places the "what" in God's capable hands at every moment and in every generation.

God can and must be trusted with outcomes. With Paul, we need to affirm confidence *"that He who began a good work in you will perform it until the day of Christ Jesus"* (Philippians 1:6).

Even more during times of real change, we must learn to examine the "how." When change is being thrust upon us, instinct and pressure make us look at the "what" and we often simply revert to our default setting for the "how."

During my years as a marriage counselor, I discovered that most marriages did not end because of issues. Often we hear that the big issues in marriage are things like sex, money, in-laws, and of course communication. But I discovered that these issues were never what did marriages in. If a marriage ended, its demise could invariably be traced to bad processes.

I discovered that no issue was irresolvable. Financial stress, difficulty with children, even unfaithfulness could all be overcome *if* married couples adopted effective processes for dealing with the issues. I discovered that the difference between marriages that survived and thrived on one hand, and those that ended or remained in constant chaos on the other was the chosen process of resolution.

Resolution is a process that looks different in every marriage, and in many cases, in every circumstance. But it is a process. Couples who could learn this process and apply it flexibly in multiple situations could overcome difficulty, and more importantly they could thrive.

One of the reasons that marriage counseling is more effective than books or conferences is that counseling allows the flexible application of a process, instead of simply delivering helpful and accurate content. The principles that make good marriages work result in processes that must be uniquely applied to unique moments and circumstances.

In effecting cultural or organizational change (as with marital change), accurate Biblical principles (content) must lead to processes that are uniquely applied to unique moments and circumstances.

For an example of process over content, read the words of the Prophet Isaiah as He speaks God's words to the nation of Israel:

> *Hear the word of the Lord, you rulers of Sodom;*
> *listen to the instruction of our God,*
> *you people of Gomorrah! "The multitude of your sacrifices—*

what are they to me?" says the Lord.
"I have more than enough of burnt offerings, of rams and the
fat of fattened animals;
I have no pleasure in the blood of bulls and lambs and goats.
When you come to appear before me,
who has asked this of you, this trampling of my courts? Stop
bringing meaningless offerings! Your incense is detestable
to me. New Moons, Sabbaths and convocations—I cannot
bear your worthless assemblies. Your New Moon feasts and
your appointed festivals I hate with all my being. They have
become a burden to me; I am weary of bearing them. When
you spread out your hands in prayer,
I hide my eyes from you;
even when you offer many prayers,
I am not listening. Your hands are full of blood!
(Isaiah 1:10-14 NIV)

Do you see the irony here? God is expressing frustration that the nation of Israel is doing all the things that He assigned them to do. They are actually following His instructions and God does not sound happy about it. Quite the contrary.

God is not frustrated with what the Israelites are doing. He is frustrated with how they are doing it. He is interested in the hearts of men, therefore He is focused on the "way" and not the "what." If we are to learn how to partner with what God is doing, and even lead in some way in His kingdom, we must learn to think not only in terms of the content that God has passed to our race, but begin to embrace how deeply God values a particular *way* of living that content.

> **"IF WE GET THE "HOW" RIGHT, IT ACTUALLY PLACES THE "WHAT" IN GOD'S CAPABLE HANDS AT EVERY MOMENT AND IN EVERY GENERATION."**

This is *the* problem in effective spiritual leadership. This is *the thing* we must consider as we survey the changing landscape of our generation.

If we can really examine not just the content of God's Word, but the processes of the Author of the Word, we may avoid the subtle trap of negotiating a season of change—changing the wrong thing. Killing cats instead of rats.

THE TRAP OF CORRECTING MISTAKES

The draw to change the wrong thing is often born of a very subtle but common mistake. Often, the changes we try to engineer are based on our best evaluation of what has been going wrong. We set out to fix what has been going wrong by setting a course correction. Far too often that course correction is a response to the course of the generation before us. The trap is that you cannot determine a correct course simply by reacting to a wrong course.

When this happens—and it happens all the time—correcting the mistakes of the previous generation actually sets the foundation for the mistakes of the next. And on the car goes, careening wildly from one highway shoulder or ditch to the other. This is not an efficient way to move forward.

In response to a generation of Charismatic excess, we might, in our corrective caution, set a course that downplays the Holy Spirit. Because one generation focused too much on intellect, the next might over-correct and overly focus on experience. While one group might presumptuously suppose to be "Spirit-led;" another might reactively presume and become righteously self-sufficient.

> "CORRECTING THE MISTAKES OF THE PREVIOUS GENERATION ACTUALLY SETS THE FOUNDATION FOR THE MISTAKES OF THE NEXT."

How do we as leaders avoid chronic "over-steer" when we clearly need to recalibrate our course? Not surprisingly, based on everything we've seen up to this point, we do so by first examining and recalibrating our process. If we try to correct what another group or generation has "done wrong" we must first consider how we will re-adjust.

Trying to diagnose the mistakes of others is a process fraught with potential pitfalls. Not only can we end up with a pendulum swing of a course change, we can also end up with a heart filled with pride and arrogance. If instead of identifying what others have done wrong, we can identify what each generation has generously given to the body, we stand a better chance of having a heart-process like the One who made us.

If we can identify the valuable contributions of any given group, we can avoid the not-so-subtle trap of criticism and comparison.

Consider for a moment if we were to develop our models of church growth and development from the letters of Paul. Clearly all scripture is God-breathed and therefore profitable for teaching and doctrine, and correction, and reproof. But just because it is inspired and inerrant does not make all scripture accurately applied by our bumbling human hands.

A passage of scripture about financial wisdom may or may not be applicable for parenting, or some other endeavor. A passage of scripture that is correcting behavior may or may not be applicable to building a ministry model. I would submit that passages that are designed to correct wrong thinking and wrong action should not be used to build models.

Imagine if your worship team showed up for rehearsal and ran through the set list, trying to identify and avoid every possible mistake in the list. Key changes and transitions provide opportunities for mistakes. Knowing this, imagine conducting a rehearsal around focusing on not making those mistakes. It doesn't make sense does it? Learn how the songs should be done, and correct mistakes if they arise.

Similarly, what if we try to negotiate change around the corrections of mistakes or errors? This will simply lead us from one set of mistakes to another. It makes more sense to develop our ministries and models around the things that Jesus did, rather than to try to negotiate change by correcting the things we have seen go wrong.

For this reason, the next several chapters will be a reexamination of the ministry and mission of Jesus. If we as leaders of the church of this century are to make any sense and any headway in this next generation, I want to recalibrate by thinking differently about the mission of Jesus, as well as the problem that Jesus came to solve.

LEADING IN TWO REALMS

Finally, another reason it is so incredibly easy to change the wrong thing is the simple yet significant fact that Christian leaders are, by definition, called to lead in two realms simultaneously.

Christianity is a belief system built upon a worldview that most westerners no longer hold. At minimum, a biblical worldview must include the understanding that we live in a world whose reality is defined by an integration of both a visible material world, and an invisible spiritual world.

While the material world is evident and easily apprised by our five senses and human reason, the spiritual world is different. The spiritual world is perceived through a different set of senses and clearly functions differently than our material world with its natural laws.

When we attempt to interpret *spiritual* things with the same tools we use to interpret *material* things—through our senses and reason—we can end up embracing a deception that feels very much like certain truth. What's more, if we do not grow in our understanding of the relationship between these two realms we may actually find that thoughts and strategies that work well in the material world can have negative impacts in the spiritual realm. Your best-crafted plans can backfire and end up being counterproductive. Mr. Foot, meet Mr. Bullet.

Imagine what the realists, skeptics and know-it-alls among the wilderness children of Israel said when they heard Joshua's plan for invading Canaan. "Say what? We're going to march around the fortress city of Jericho a bunch of times and then shout and blow horns? Really?" And "Um ... hey, Joshua ... there's this thing called the laws of physics. Perhaps you've heard of them." The fact is, when it comes to mastering the things of the spiritual realm, being an expert in material things can be a profound disadvantage.

In my life's assignment to help people find personal freedom, I have found that some of the most difficult people to help are those who excel in the material realm. People who are very good at *Earth* stuff may actually be quite impaired in their functioning in the invisible kingdom stuff. In a realm where dying equals true life and giving away leads to true wealth, people who can only see one half of the equation struggle greatly to operate in the duality of the material and the spiritual realms.

Now add to this the idea that we often recognize and validate leadership qualities based on how well people succeed on *Earth*. The outcome of this formula is that we often promote to kingdom leadership those who have succeeded in only one realm. A man or woman's ability to succeed at Earth, may or may not tell us anything about their ability to succeed in two realms simultaneously. In fact, in many cases this can be a set up for promoting people and instilling leaders who struggle deeply in their true understanding of, and effective action in, the invisible Kingdom of God.

Simply acknowledging the presence of the spiritual realm is not enough. We can have a materialistic worldview and apply it to an understanding that a spiritual realm exists. Much of our legalistic thought process and harmful charismatic practices (not to be confused with healthy charismatic practices) can be a direct result of acknowledging that a spiritual realm exists but applying naturalistic and humanistic thought process to that view. Many of our harmful practices can also come from investing deeply in the natural realm, but being entirely unfamiliar with the spiritual realm.

To lead effectively in any Christian endeavor requires a growing awareness of and developing healthy practices for interacting in both a natural and a spiritual realm. To lead effectively in the Church we must grow in our understanding of how these two worlds relate, and how our actions and interactions influence this relationship.

> **"CHRISTIANITY IS A BELIEF SYSTEM BUILT UPON A WORLDVIEW THAT MOST WESTERNERS NO LONGER HOLD."**

To whom can we look for this kind of insight? Who can mentor us in living successfully and simultaneously in two realms? Who indeed.

A PARABLE— PART II

The Teacher pondered how the motorcycle had been received this last week. All the appropriate oohs and ahhs had been uttered. The buzz was there. Even his friend down the street had been hearing about the moment the roar reverberated through his gathering.

He should be thinking about next week, but instead his thoughts went backward. He, along with all the Master Teachers, was well versed in the History of The Game. It was a particular area of great strength for him. Strategy and History had been his emphasis in school. Today he pondered History.

The Game had been invented by a Man who taught an entire village to play. Or at least the entire village had *seen* the first game. In that day, the buzz had been all about the Greatest Game ever invented.

Those who played and those who watched had all recognized that something big was happening. The Man had gathered all those who would play in mid-field and began to show them how to play.

This was not your average game. Those who gathered on the sidelines all knew this was the beginning of something.

Though not all played, all wanted to be a part of something big. So the spectators found ways to participate. Some developed cheers and chants to encourage the players. Others began to write down the rules and strategies so The Game could be reproduced in other villages.

It was this group that had eventually developed a training program, spawning the elite group of Master Teachers. Thoroughly educated and well versed in the History, the Master Teachers knew The Game through and through.

Today, like the first day, none of them had actually *played* The Game. But they knew everything there was to know about it.

CHAPTER 3

THE MISSION OF JESUS

"Maybe we've been living with our eyes half open. Maybe we're bent and broken."
—Switchfoot, We Were Meant to Live

"These walls are funny. First you hate 'em. Then you get used to 'em. Enough time passes, you get so you depend on 'em."
—The Shawshank Redemption

Change. Rapid, convulsive, dizzying change. As in no other period in history, change characterizes the days in which we're living.

Supposedly the ancient Chinese had a special curse they would pronounce upon a despised enemy. It was: "May you live in *interesting* times." Well, the days in which we're living have become downright fascinating. Every major system in the world around us is seemingly in flux. Volatile economies, unstable governments ... even the planet itself seems restless, groaning in an intensifying state of upheaval.

In the midst of this chaos we have the Church—struggling to comprehend and respond. Indeed, much of the institution we call the Church appears badly in need of an overhaul. Sure, some churches are exploding with growth, but many others are experiencing a mass exodus. Whole mainline traditions are crumbling—some seeing their leaders fall or falter amid a series of scandals. Other once-great denominations have sacrificed their vital distinctiveness on the altar of political correctness in a misguided quest to remain "relevant" (a.k.a. changing the wrong thing). They are a withering shell of their former selves.

One friend of mine says people are leaving their churches because they are trying to find God. What an ironic thing. And sad.

Change is a given. We can't opt out. What remains for us as Christian leaders then is to learn to be wise stewards of what is taking place in our time. As for me, thinking about change and how to navigate well in the midst of it is one of my favorite topics. This subject fascinates me because epochs of epic change invariably present us with significant forks in the road—opportunities to go the right way or the wrong way. During my 16 years as a family therapist my job was to engage families in the midst of crisis and help them choose the right way instead of the wrong way—to change the right thing.

As I mentioned, when I look at the Church, it seems to me we're in a bit of a crisis. We're not handling this era of epic change so well. And as one who has seen up close the damage and heartache that changing the wrong thing can cause—whether to families or churches—it bothers me.

That burden birthed this book. I'm keenly, passionately interested in learning to navigate and engineer change in the church world and change in individuals. Let's learn to be agents of the right kind of change in these exciting and volatile times. Why? Because the leaders of the Church today will determine the position, power, and health of the Church tomorrow.

As we observed in the previous chapter, in times of rapid transformation one of the great temptations the Church faces is to change the wrong thing. But it's not the only pitfall. Some are drawn to finding new ways to repackage the same old things in an attempt to address the problems of modernity. We might even be urged to imitate the world's system by coming up with clever marketing strategies to persuade and motivate people. We may also be tempted to look to the culture around us for models of leadership and cultural relevance. These counterfeits for meaningful, appropriate, effective change tempt us because they actually *seem* to be the right thing to do. But the thing that makes them even more seductive is that the need for change is so urgent. The fog of crisis clouds our vision and impairs our judgment.

How do we avoid these pitfalls and stay on the path that leads to beneficial change? We do so by avoiding a couple of deadly flaws.

The first is the mistake of making changes at the wrong level. Allow me to explain.

ORDERS OF CHANGE

In change theory (that's right, some very smart academic types have spent a lot of time studying how organizations move, grow and change), there is a concept of orders or levels of change.

Any change within an organization or entity can be generally classified as a First Order, Second Order, or Third Order change—depending upon how deep, transformative and consequential the change is. The higher the order, the more transformative and consequential the change.

First order change—for both individuals and organizations—merely improves upon what already is. It's tweak-y. It usually consists of finding ways to do things a little better, faster or easier. Change of the first order can result in modest, incremental improvements (provided the right thing has been changed). To illustrate with a sports example (can you tell I'm fond of those?), first order change is like if I were a basketball coach who determines in the middle of a game that my current approach isn't working. The scoreboard says so. So I switch from zone defense to man-to-man. Or I make a personnel substitution or two. In other words, I make a change that I hope will make things work better.

It's the same game, being played with the same objective and by the same rules. I've just tweaked my approach. It's cosmetics, not structure. Content, not processes. This is first order change.

Second order change is a more fundamental type, often involving the creation of something new. In organizations, second order change is characterized by structural change that requires cultivating a new culture and a new way of thinking. In other words, the new structure will usually clash with the old beliefs and habits. So, a new set of beliefs and habits is necessary in order to function in the new system.

Returning to my basketball team illustration, say that during the off-season we decided to change the rules in some fundamental ways. That has certainly happened in the past with the addition of the shot clock and the three-point line. When these changes took effect, it had a huge impact on the way the game was played as well as the strategies employed to attain victory. For the players, long-held, deeply ingrained habits had to be unlearned. New habits had to be cultivated and new thinking adopted. The change went beyond content to process. That's the nature of second order change.

Whereas first order change is incremental and consists of improving what already is, second order change is more fundamental and consists of creating a new set of beliefs that make possible behavior that had been impossible before.

30

When it comes to "fixing" things, improving things and affecting change, most of us spend all of our time and energies in the realm of the first order. This is true both for us as individuals and as Christian organizational leaders. The first level is where most of us live.

Here's a practical example drawn from my years of marriage and family counseling practice. Let's take a hypothetical married couple that has chronic conflict. Let's say you've tried and tried to help them resolve the conflict. You've given them all the best conflict resolution tools. You've walked them through the strategies for handling anger. You've tried to give them everything you know to change it. But for some reason the pattern of fighting stubbornly persists.

All of this, by definition, lies in the realm of first order change because it's all about strategy adjustment and substituting one response for another. It doesn't address the rules of the "game" they're playing. But what if there is an unwritten rule in their home that says, "The only way husband and wife ever deeply connect is after a fight?" There are many couples who only know how to have intimacy in the context of a post-fight makeup. It's a fairly common dynamic. (How many references in movies and television sitcoms have you heard about "make-up sex" recently?)

Thus the couple—no matter how well equipped with information and strategies (content) they are—continues to experience conflict because it's structurally integrated via the unspoken rules of the relationship. The rule is: Something both parties in the relationship desperately want, i.e., intimacy, only comes after engaging in something that you really hate, fighting. You have to do *this* in order to have that.

First order change will never solve a structural problem like this. Until you change that rule, the fighting must continue. And rewriting rules only happens in the realm of second order change.

Again and again and again in human systems—whether marriages, families, or organizations such as local churches—attempts at change fail because the change is taking place at the wrong level. Everywhere I look in the Church, I see us making heroic, herculean efforts to fix or improve the ways we reach people and disciple people and impact our communities, but largely doing so exclusively in the realm of first order change. Rarely, if ever, does anyone ask the question, "Are we changing the right thing? And at the right level?" It's a process issue, not a content issue. Until we move beyond the first level of change, no matter what sparkly new innovation the Church rolls out or old tradition it resurrects, she will simply be rearranging the deck chairs on the Titanic.

So, what about third order change? Change at this level goes still farther and deeper than rule-changes and restructuring of process, actually leaving rigid rule following and brittle structure behind. Third order change is mission directed rather than rule directed. It requires walking away from the Tree of the Knowledge of Good and Evil (more on this in a subsequent chapter).

When we look back at our own attempts to "do church" throughout the generations we see us making adjustments to our approach. Some adjustments are in our presentation, such as moving from hymns to worship choruses, and from hymnals to PowerPoint slides. Sometimes we see that we adjust our orthodoxy in an attempt to be more effective. Some will tighten the orthodoxy to be sure that we maintain our saltiness and doctrinal purity. Others will try to loosen the bounds of orthodoxy in order to be more palatable, or relevant to changing culture. These groups then begin to respond and react to each other, each pointing out the others' weaknesses, and adjusting their stances and responses to counter the other.

The difficulty here is that the change of "style" and even the adjustments of tightening or loosening our orthodoxy are all first order change. We are adjusting the offense or defense, without consideration of the possibility for a higher order.

> **"WHENEVER WE VIEW THE THINGS OF GOD THROUGH THE LENS OF MEN, WE HAVE ALREADY MISUNDERSTOOD."**

When Jesus is approached in Matthew 22:23-33 by the Sadducees in order to test Him, they ask Him a question. They tell the story of the seven brothers who married the same woman and each die (I call this the parable of the unwise brothers). They then ask a question about how this plays out in eternity. Jesus' answer is paradigm shifting.

He says, "You are mistaken, not understanding the scriptures and the Power of God ..." and then goes on to deliver the rest of the answer. But the real and most important answer has already been delivered in this phrase. The men gathered did not understand the Scriptures (nor do you or I, I might add), in light of the Power of God. In other words, we view the scriptures from the Earth looking up, instead of from Heaven looking down. Whenever we view the things of God through the lens of men, we have already misunderstood. Like trying to understand an elephant with a microscope, our paradigm will not allow an accurate view of our subject.

Our orthodoxy can be a completely accurate set of gathered doctrines, but viewed through an Earthly lens, we will always reduce it to something less than its fullness. We can see our doctrines as a rule to be ruthlessly followed regardless of context, or a rule too rigid to accurately represent the Love of God. Both can be the wrong view, because we look not through the lens of "the Power of God" but rather through the lens of Earthly application.

The Kingdom of Heaven is not only the Presence of God on the Earth to act on behalf of God and man, it is a paradigm through which our orthodoxy always makes perfect and compassionate sense. If it is not making sense or seems too dogmatic, the problem is not the doctrines that we have held so dear, it is the paradigm through which we view our orthodoxy. There is a paradigm intended to govern our orthodoxy that is qualitatively different from that which the human race has been born into.

When we adjust our styles and presentations, or even adjust the parameters of the standards of our faith (in either direction), we are making first order change. When we allow a higher order or a higher perspective to give us a new view of the same parameters or stylistic approaches, second order change occurs; and instead of adjusting our approach, we ourselves are adjusted as we choose to know the Scriptures through the lens of the Power and perspective of God, instead of our own ability and knowledge.

We must view all of our expressions of doctrine and church through the worldview that includes both a visible and an invisible world. With this in mind we are much more likely to identify and change the right thing.

A third order organization operates from questions rather than answers. A third order *church* asks questions such as, "What is the voice of God saying today?" And, "How does our mission harmonize with the mission of Jesus?"

So many are dissatisfied with continuing on in the same rut, just doing church as it has been done as long as they can remember. They voice common complaints: Christians are judgmental; church is boring or seems ineffective. The Church is seen by many as irrelevant, or even worse, as a destructive force in our culture.

The emperor has been declared naked, yet many are trying to get him to act "dressed." So the temptation is to modernize by taking our cues from the culture and our ideas from the latest trendy gurus in the world of business. Don't get me wrong. I'm not against striving for cultural relevancy. I'm just urging us not to mistake cultural relevancy for the real change that is needed. The changes we make to be "relevant" are almost always first-order changes.

Here's a key point: we don't just want to examine how to change or fine-tune our strategy; we also need to question if our strategy is aimed at the right target. If we take a look at the larger picture and examine the question, "Are we really fulfilling the mission that Jesus came to give us?" it will help us move toward a higher order of change.

This is the first of the two pitfalls I mentioned above—making change at the wrong level. And that second pitfall? It is …

CORRECTING THE MISTAKES OF THE PAST

There's a derisive old saying about military leaders—namely, that the present generation of Generals and Admirals are always doggedly preparing to fight the *last* war, rather then the next one. At the heart of this criticism is the recognition of our very human tendency to let the problems of the past blind us to the real solutions of the present and future.

This temptation is particularly powerful in times of change. Often our adjustments are little more than a reactive response to perceived mistakes of past generations, rather than strategic changes for the proactive purpose of establishing what is right. If all we do is look one or two generations back and try to make corrections where we believe the Church has gone astray, we're likely to end up simply swinging the pendulum back toward the other extreme. But that approach rarely changes the right thing at the right level.

This is a strange but easily understood phenomenon. Easy, because people instinctively react to discomfort. When something causes us pain, we're hardwired to move away from the source and seek comfort. What is true for us as individuals is equally true for organizations or communities. Or movements.

Here is how the pendulum dynamic has operated in the Church in the past. When one generation of churches seemed boring and lifeless, the next became intentional about being more passionate. If the previous generation of Charismatics was viewed as weird and flakey, then the one that follows will scrupulously avoid seeking any and all modern-day manifestations of God's presence for fear of being labeled weird and flakey. Did the last generation turn people off by becoming too heady or intellectual? Then let's reject anything that smacks of intellectualism and focus on experience.

Here is one of the reactions du jour: "Christians have been too judgmental. So, let's throw away the things that are hard for people to hear. Let's soften our teaching."

I frequently see this dynamic demonstrated in the ways people develop doctrinal stances or ministry models. Quite often people build a church or ministry approach based on the letters of Paul the Apostle. His letters are filled with great doctrine, so it would only make sense to build around his thinking and approach ... except for one major problem: Paul's writings are often designed to correct mistakes or problems in the newly developing First Century Church. Therefore, if those portions of Paul's writings form the basis for how we think of doctrinal development and ministry approaches, then we will be building on a foundation of correcting mistakes.

We cannot build a right thing from a blueprint that consists only of correcting a wrong thing.

Where can we find a better blueprint? It's been hiding in plain sight in the Gospels and the opening chapters of Genesis. We need to take notice of what Jesus did and what He explained about why He did it. Put another way, we need to pattern what we do according to God's *original* design—not according to His inspired correction of human mistakes. For if we build our approaches solely

> **"IF WE BUILD OUR APPROACHES SOLELY ON MISTAKE CORRECTION, WE MAY FIND THE ONLY THING WE'RE REALLY GOOD AT IS POINTING OUT WHAT OTHERS DO WRONG."**

on mistake correction, we may find the only thing we're really good at is pointing out what others do wrong. We may never find the time, skill or resources to help others learn and grow.

That would be a terrible place to end up.

JESUS' APPROACH

There were times when Jesus taught in a synagogue or spoke to a crowd on a hillside, but His ministry could not be characterized as a classroom approach, and it was far more than a simple motivational device. Jesus walked with normal people through the struggles of normal life, and He delivered the power and presence of God to anyone who would receive. In Acts 10:38, the essence of His mission and ministry are described this way:

> *You know of Jesus of Nazareth, how God anointed Him with the Holy Spirit and with power, and how He went about doing good and healing all who were oppressed by the devil, for God was with Him.* (NASB)

The emphasis in that statement is not merely on the things done, but also highlights the truth that the gospel is something living and active, not simply a topic for study, analysis and reflection. A ditch exists on either side of that dynamic. If we lean too far toward the *learning* side, we become inactive and discipleship is reduced to mere cognition. If we lean too far toward the *doing* side, then we can narrow the whole issue of change down to being "missional."

At the risk of dismaying my passionately missional friends (and they are many), the current emphasis on missional-ity in the Church seems to be an over-reaction to the previous trap, landing us in another ditch. The concept of the Church being an agent for social change is a context, but should not be an emphasis. A group can be missional (involved in many worthy outreaches), yet be just as self-generated as the intellectual crowd.

"A GROUP CAN BE MISSIONAL YET BE JUST AS SELF-GENERATED AS THE INTELLECTUAL CROWD."

Jesus taught in the midst of His activity. He trained as He worked. This is the key to understanding the active nature of the gospel. The issue here is not only the activity, but that His *method* was absolutely congruent with His *message*. Simply being active was not the message itself, but rather the essential context for His message. If His message had been characterized by a classroom-style delivery, then it would have become a different message—void of the results described in Acts 10:38.

The truth is, if the core of our discipleship program involves sitting around talking, we shouldn't be surprised if our disciples only sit around and talk.

As we try to wade through the changes ahead, some of our methods should change; but the method of change is not the point or the goal. The method should change to become congruent with the message itself. Since the method should be an outgrowth of the message, it would be a mistake to examine the method only without first re-examining the message. (We'll examine that message with fresh eyes in the next chapter.)

THE MISSION

Before we begin to really dig into the message of Jesus, let's look at His mission. For too long we have believed that Jesus came to motivate the lazy, educate the ignorant, and correct the wayward. But let's take a look at His mission through the eyes of Scripture.

I won't take time to quote the lengthy passage here, but Romans 5:12-21 describes a simple concept in multiple ways. In short, what was lost to the human race through Adam was restored through Christ. Everything that was polluted or destroyed through Adam's rebellion was regained through the life and actions of Jesus. We see this truth echoed in the book of Luke when Jesus utters these words:

> *"For the Son of Man has come to seek and to save that which was lost."* (Luke 19:10, NASB)

The context of this verse is the story of Zacchaeus—the guy Jesus noticed up in the tree above the heads of the crowd. But the statement refers to much more that was lost besides the soul of a tax collector. Jesus was describing the original sinless nature of man that was lost when Adam sinned. He also alludes to the effect the Fall had upon the condition of the whole Earth. Jesus' mission was to restore all things to their original glorious state God had intended. It is partly our lack of awareness of this original state that makes us so prone to make the gospel about behavior management.

John Eldredge, in his excellent book *Waking the Dead*, makes a point that has become one of my favorites. He says we talk so much of original sin; yet we forget that before Adam sinned, we lived in a state of original glory. Remembering God's original design, rather than man's original sin, can help us do more than simply correct the broken things we see in front of us. Jesus did not come to simply correct our behavior. He came to restore a lost state of *being*. Before the fall of man, God looked at us and pronounced us "very good."

The first and most important way to understand the mission of Jesus is to consider it a recovery mission. Jesus has come to restore His Father's original design to creation, and people are part of His creation.

IMMANUEL: GOD WITH US

Another significant part of God's design has to do with His dwelling place. In Eden, it was as natural as breathing for God and man to live together on this planet. They walked and talked in the Garden together, occasionally naming some animals along the way. God and man were partners in ruling over Creation.

In Isaiah, we find one of the most appealing and meaningful names assigned to Jesus. In prophesying of His coming to Earth, Isaiah tells us:

> *Therefore the Lord Himself will give you a sign: Behold, a virgin will be with child and bear a son, and she will call His name Immanuel.* (Isaiah 7:14, NASB)

We associate the name Immanuel—which means "God with us"—with Christmas because we sing the name in songs that celebrate His birth. Of course, that birth indeed marks the restoration of God living with men. (Once again, His mission is *restoration*.) Ever since the first Christ-mas, God has dwelt on Earth with men. For a season, He did so in the physical body of Jesus. Then when Jesus ascended, He sent the Holy Spirit to operate as the designated representative of the Godhead on Earth. This restoration of God's presence with us is one of the most significant parts of Jesus' mission, because every other part of the restoration process flows out of His presence among His people.

The truth that Adam and Eve lived via an ongoing, life-giving connection to God, who was present with them, is central to understanding the original glory (the state of man before the Fall). Living in God's Presence is a bit like living in the presence of fire. The very nearness of it creates things like heat, energy, comfort, and safety. It is not simply that God likes to be around people; it is that His Being is the source of everything we need. God being with us is also central to the next description of Jesus' mission.

IT WAS FOR FREEDOM

It is worth devoting a few pages to the subject of freedom at this point. I am convinced the Bible can provide a picture of freedom very different from the one most of us carry around in our heads. As Galatians 5:1 states concisely and clearly, *"It is for freedom that Christ has set us free"* (NIV). If we do not place the concept of freedom squarely at the head of Jesus' "to do" list, we will miss the whole thing! And His presence remains the key to this facet of His mission. Note that Second Corinthians 3:17 tells us, *"Where the Spirit of the Lord is, there is freedom"* (NIV).

When Jesus stood up in the synagogue and proclaimed His personal mission statement, He said:

> *"The Spirit of the LORD is upon Me, because He anointed Me to preach the gospel to the poor. He has sent Me to proclaim release to the captives, and recovery of sight to the blind, to set free those who are downtrodden, to proclaim the favorable year of the Lord."* (Luke 4:18-19, NASB)

This proclamation declares what Jesus came to do for people, not what He expects people to do for Him. In it you will find no contempt or scorn for the lazy or the ignorant. Instead, there is compassion for those who are trapped, and a militant response to the captors. Jesus' mission was to help us. Freedom is the natural result.

Previously, I pointed us to the opening chapters of the Bible for vital insight on Jesus' mission and message. The dividing line between the first three chapters of Genesis and the rest of the Bible narrative is a significant one. We must draw from those chapters every bit of evidence we can for God's original design. I am convinced that most of us define freedom from a post-Genesis-Chapter-3 perspective and as a result are pursuing something far lower than what is available to us.

Everyone born after Genesis 3 was born into a prison. This prison affected our minds and limited our thinking. As a result, we all suffer from a perspective that I call "prisoner thinking"—the thought processes formed when we have no other experience but our own from which to draw.

Consider a child born in a prison camp. He is raised behind the gray walls, razor wire fences and dirt floors of the compound. As he grows, he learns to yearn, along with his fellow prisoners, for "freedom." He stands at the fences and stares out at the world beyond his prison walls. Ask him what he wants, and he would say, "Freedom." However, his mental trap is revealed when he attempts to answer the question: "What is freedom?"

"Freedom," he might say, "means not living here; it means not eating this food and not having to answer to the guards. It means living out there." His frustrated gesture would draw one's attention to the land beyond the fence. And even though he knows that he wants to be "out there," the only thing he really knows is "in here."

He has never played soccer on a green field. He has never run on a beach and plunged into the water. He has never climbed a mountain, dated the girl next door, or bought his first car. His definition of freedom is entirely built upon what would not be happening, because he has absolutely no idea what is possible. He has no way of knowing what he doesn't know. Prisoners think that freedom is the absence of something. The absence of bars, the absence of obstacles, the absence of forced regimentation, the absence of fear or insecurity … these are the ways we think about freedom.

This is where we must return to examine the mind-set of a typical Christian. We, too, have learned to think like prisoners. Freedom, we believe, will come when I am no longer angry, when I get my habit under control, when I no longer have this addiction. Can you see how this is also prisoner thinking? The Bible is very clear that freedom is not the absence of something; it is the presence of *Someone*. Remember? Where the Spirit of the Lord is … there is freedom.

Freedom is not about the control of impulse and behavior; it is about the fulfillment of identity and destiny. Your identity and destiny cannot be restored apart from the presence of God on Earth. Freedom is about being restored to live life as the man or woman that God created and redeemed you to be. It is not about just limiting the bad things, but instead it is about unleashing the good things for which you were made.

TO TEAR THE VEIL

The final aspect of Jesus' mission is just as important as the others I have mentioned. In fact, these issues are so intertwined that you cannot separate one aspect of His mission from another. For men to be free and live free, God must be present; for God to be present, a re-connection must take place between the two realms in which we were intended to simultaneously live.

In John 3:11-13, Jesus declares that He has occupied both the Heavens and the Earth. He stands in front of Nicodemus and says, "You don't even believe Me when I tell you about Earthly things. How will you believe when I tell you about Heavenly things?" Jesus' declaration of the kingdom of Heaven coming among men was not a declaration of commandments, rules, and regulations; it was a declaration of two realms coming together. Throughout His Earthly ministry, He both proclaimed and demonstrated that Heaven and Earth should not be separate, but together. Heaven comes to a leper, and he is cleansed. Heaven comes to a tax collector, and his heart becomes generous. Jesus speaks to a dead body, the Breath of Heaven moves in, and the dead body rises.

When the two realms intersect, the eternal realm restores to the Earthly realm its original design. When Jesus is crucified, the veil hanging in the Temple is torn in two from top to bottom. This veil has been separating the realm of God from the realm of man. When the veil is torn, the next recorded activity is that the bodies of the saints buried around Jerusalem rose from the grave and began to share the good news of the Kingdom.

An essential aspect of Jesus' ministry was proclaiming and demonstrating the possibility of this intersection of the Heavenly and Earthly realms. For Jesus to seek and to save all that was lost, He had to rescue the realm of Earth from its fate of existing so separately from the realm that is the source of all things eternal.

As we have seen, Jesus' mission was to set captives free. Since Genesis 3, men and women have lived in a prison constructed of a *way* of thinking. I don't mean just

"THE BIBLE IS VERY CLEAR THAT FREEDOM IS NOT THE ABSENCE OF SOMETHING; IT IS THE PRESENCE OF SOMEONE."

that they think bad thoughts. I am saying they have a fallen way of thinking all their thoughts—both good and bad. This is why people end up angry, or starving, or addicted, or living in poverty. The outward expressions of this mental prison are almost unlimited in their variety. When we try to respond to these expressions of bondage (poverty, addictions, human trafficking, abuse and countless others) without actually setting captives free, we fail to really fulfill the mission of Jesus. We can be missionally successful in carrying out the wrong mission.

Freedom was *the* mission of Jesus. He came to set us free from anything that restrains us from fulfilling our God-given destiny. And He freed us from anything that prevents us from becoming the person we were created to be. Disease, demonic oppression, selfishness—all of these enemies of the human soul are subject to Jesus' strategy. But the mission was far more than removing these obstacles. The mission was to open a way for men and women to be who they were made to be and do what they were made to do, and to live in that zone of intersection between Heaven and here.

However, if we are to grasp the true scope of the nature of human bondage, we must move beyond understanding Jesus' mission to understanding the very specific problem that Jesus came to solve.

"THE GAME"

A PARABLE— PART III

Those who had first recognized the immense value of The Game were also in some ways the ones who had inadvertently conspired to keep it hidden. They didn't mean to. In fact, in many ways, they had hoped to promote The Game and convince the world of its value. They knew it was important. But they were missing one thing. They had not played The Game on that very first day.

For all of the buzz, they could see that something significant was unfolding in front of them. It was this sense of value that had led them to begin to write down what they saw and learned.

What they could not see was that which was only evident out on the field itself. Like any sport, participation is the greatest teacher. And The Game was no different. In fact, this Game was so uniquely developed that most of the impact could only be experienced on the field.

The beauty of teamwork, the strength of seeing from on the field, the way that strategy unfolded from the movement of the team and the ball. The Game almost taught itself—if you were on the field. Not only did it teach itself, it seemed to change the participants.

This Game was unlike any other. Those who wrote down what they saw intended to preserve and promote it. In many ways their passion for promoting The Game began to obscure The Game itself.

Without even realizing it, they laid the very foundation that would undermine it. If it could in fact have been undermined.

CHAPTER 4

THE PROBLEM JESUS CAME TO SOLVE

"Ground control to major Tom. Your circuit's dead, there's something wrong. Can you hear me, major Tom?"
—David Bowie, Space Oddity

"What gets us into trouble is not what we don't know. It's what we do know for sure that just ain't so."
—Mark Twain

The most significant life ever lived—and the most important sacrifice made by any man in human history—could be wasted. That's right. In a sense, all that Jesus was and all He accomplished could be squandered *if* we don't accurately understand *why* He did it. What a tragedy it would be if we wandered off the path laid out by the life, death and resurrection of Jesus the Christ. Yet, the very problem that He came to solve makes it extremely likely that we could miss it. And not just by a little bit. We *could* miss the importance and intent of His life, death, and resurrection—by a mile!

In all my years of counseling, perhaps the most helpful insight I applied was this one: defining problems correctly is the key to successful change. I often joked that I would always have job security as long as people continued to define their problems incorrectly.

Around the turn of the last century, G.K. Chesterton said, "It isn't that they can't see the solution. It's that they can't see the problem." One hundred years later Stephen Covey echoed Chesterton when he wrote: "The way we see the problem is the problem." It's true. The way we define our problems directly impacts how we respond to them. And these definitions particularly impact the solutions we choose to implement (for better or worse), as well as the ways we think about those solutions.

Our definitions set our minds and, therefore, our course. And the most important and impacting definition we carry is our definition of the human condition; or put another way, whether or not we understand the problem Jesus came to solve.

At first, it seems like an easy thing to define. "What is the problem Jesus came to solve?" We think the answer to this question has been made abundantly clear. Many learned it in Sunday School. In fact, we know it so well that the answer leaps into our minds with almost the same involuntary response as when we blink at a sudden movement.

However, the very fact that our answer to the question is instinctive makes it all the more important to stop a moment and consider the question more carefully. You see, our instincts come from our natural inclinations and thought processes that are inherently, deeply shaped by the very problem Jesus came to solve. These same instincts might cause you to stop after the next few sentences, put down this book and immediately brand me a heretic.

I implore you to stay with me to see if your presuppositions have, to some degree, clouded the very issue that Jesus came to clarify and conquer. Are you ready?

When asked, "What problem did Jesus come to solve?" the answer that comes to our mind so naturally is the "S" word—*Sin*. Right? And of course, in a sense Jesus *did* come to solve the problem of sin ... but now comes the dilemma. The chapter in the Bible that most clearly lays out this problem never once mentions the word sin. Nope, not once. The third chapter of Genesis tells the story of the fall of man—how Adam and Eve ate the forbidden fruit from the Tree of the Knowledge of Good and Evil. Yet nowhere in that entire chapter does the word sin appear, not in any of its forms, in either English or Hebrew.

That's right, the chapter in the Bible that describes the very event and resulting condition that necessitated Jesus' journey to Earth, His death, and His resurrection never once uses the word "sin."

Are you okay? Stay with me and I believe any concerns or tension you might have will be resolved. However, I must warn you that I might create another kind of tension altogether.

ONE EVENT WITH TWO PROBLEMS

The events recorded in Genesis 3 changed more about us than we realize. In fact, one of the most destructive effects of the Fall was the impact it had on our whole process of "realizing." We might be aware of some of the problems that this event caused, but we seldom are aware of the number of *bad solutions* that have resulted from it. Allow me to illustrate how this works.

Over the years, I have become increasingly dependent on corrective glasses. In particular, my distance vision has become blurred. I purchased a pair of glasses that are relatively invisible. They have clear frames and are very light. I chose them with the hope that they would not be very visible to others when I wear them. Unfortunately, this is also true when I lay them down somewhere in my house—they are not very easy for *me* to spot. On several occasions over the last few years I have misplaced my glasses. When that happens I have two significant and related problems.

The first problem is the evident one: my glasses are missing. I have lost something of value and utility that I carry with me every day, like my keys and my wallet. I can perceive this problem easily and immediately. The second challenge is less evident; however, in many ways it is a more serious problem than the first. The first problem is that I lost something. The second is this: *The WAY I find lost things is the very thing I have lost.*

> **"IN THE MOMENT THEY CONSUMED THE FRUIT FROM THE TREE OF THE KNOWLEDGE OF GOOD AND EVIL, THEY LOST A THING AND THEY LOST A WAY."**

My glasses give me the ability to see so that I can find lost things; but that ability, that *way* of finding things, is the thing I need to find. I have lost a way of finding lost things.

This is exactly the difficulty encountered by Adam and Eve after their fateful choice. In the moment they consumed the fruit from the Tree of the Knowledge of Good and Evil, they lost a thing *and* they lost a way. God had warned them they would lose their lives. He was not just warning them about losing their immortality; He was letting them know that their spirit would lose its connection to Him, the Source of True Life.

But I want to suggest another outcome of the Fall. The same moment they lost their living connection with God, they also lost their way of perceiving what they had lost and therefore of finding it. They didn't just lose a what. They lost a way.

HOW WE KNOW

How we know something is of more importance than *what* we know. (Remember our discussion of process over content?) Don't miss the weight of this thought: we spend a great deal of time helping people know the right things, but we seldom consider helping people know things in the right way. This may shock you, but even the very Truth of God can be known in a way that brings death instead of life. In Jesus' day, the Pharisees demonstrated again and again how their knowledge of the Scriptures could still be used to bring death.

Paul prays for the Ephesian church that God would open the eyes of their heart that they might *know* things that can be understood only by the Spirit of God (Ephesians 1:18 and 1 Corinthians 2:12-16). Paul knows that their physical eyes, along with the rest of their physical senses, may learn a right thing; but then that information can be interpreted by their natural mind in a wrong way. Jesus was not just the Truth and the Life. He was also something crucial to how we understand the Truth and the Life: He was the Way. Let's go back and look at the set up.

Adam was a man who came into being like no other. He began as a ball of dirt taken from the ground. That ball of dirt had no personality, no emotions, no cognition, and no reasoning process. It had no senses or insecurities. It was just dirt. It had no opinions or perceptions. It was just dirt.

Then something amazing happened. God formed and sculpted this dirt according to His own likeness. Then the Bible says that God breathed into it the "Breath of Life" so that the man became a living soul. This means that he became a *self.* His self-hood, his opinions, his identity, his perceptions, and his reasoning processes all came from his Source. They came to him through and from the Breath of Life.

Man's origin, his roots, and his ongoing sense of self-hood came from God through the Spirit of Life that God had breathed into him. God's Breath was not only Adam's source of life, but also his source of living—in an ongoing sense. It became his source of thinking and knowing. But here is the most important point: the Breath of Life provided Adam's *way* of seeing and knowing—it was the very foundation for *how* he lived.

SEEING MORE THAN THE FOREST AND THE TREES

God did not just put life and thought inside Adam; He put His own Spirit/ Breath inside of him so that Adam could process and understand the world around him in the same way God does. Adam and Eve had a *way of knowing* that was quite different from our own. They even had a *way of seeing* that was quite different from our own. Notice this in the Genesis account:

> *And out of the ground the* LORD *God caused to grow every tree that is pleasing to the sight and good for food; the tree of life also in the midst of the garden, and the tree of the knowledge of good and evil.* (Genesis 2:9, NASB)

If we read these words with fresh eyes, it is almost as if the writer is setting the scene. I believe he is. But look closely at the scene. Slow down and read it again. In this astounding verse, the writer describes some common, everyday objects that have some startling, not-so-common characteristics.

First, the verse describes trees. You've seen trees. Trees are a familiar part of our everyday life, so we know what they look like. And we have clear mental concepts of fruit growing on trees. But how many of us have ever *seen* life? How many of us have ever *seen* knowledge? I would submit that none of us have ever seen these things. We may have seen *signs* of life and *evidence* of knowledge, but we have never seen actual life and actual knowledge.

Adam and Eve had a *way* of seeing. They had a way of knowing. And that way gave them visual access to things that you and I have never seen. To them, life and knowledge were so visible and tangible that they could reach out and touch them—not just touch them, they could pick them, hold them, take a bite and swallow them!

Adam and Eve lived in a world that was an integration of what we would call the visible and the invisible world. They would not use those distinctions because it was all visible to them. It was all visible because the way they knew and interacted with everything was *by the Spirit*. Therefore, they regularly and naturally saw things in their environment that we have never seen.

Here's our problem ... Because we see all that we see, we think what we see is all there is. More specifically, we think that if our physical eyes see what is around us, then we have seen all there is to see. Jesus never fell into the trap of making that assumption.

SOME CANNOT SEE THAT THEY CANNOT SEE

According to the record of the Gospels, Jesus never encountered a blind person that He didn't heal. But how many of the tens of thousands of people Jesus encountered were blind?

In a sense, the answer is "all of them!"

> And Jesus said, "For judgment I came into this world, so that those who do not see may see, and that those who see may become blind." Those of the Pharisees who were with Him heard these things and said to Him, 'We are not blind too, are we?' Jesus said to them, "If you were blind, you would have no sin; but since you say, 'We see,' your sin remains."
> (John 9:39-41, NASB)

Jesus never met a man or woman who was not blind. The distinction is that some of the blind people He met knew they were blind and asked to see, and some believed they had sight so they refused to receive.

Adam and Eve's way of knowing things (as is true with every way of knowing) extended beyond simply how their senses took in reality. A way of knowing also has to do with how reality is processed: what the mind does with data once it enters through the senses.

As stated earlier, *how* we know, matters more than *what* we know. We find a clear example of this in the life of the Pharisees. We know that the Pharisees knew the scriptures better than almost anyone. After all, that was a major requirement to become a Pharisee. But something about those guys led Jesus to say things like this:

"HOW WE KNOW SOMETHING IS OF MORE IMPORTANCE THAN WHAT WE KNOW."

> "You travel around the world to make a convert and when you do, you make him twice the sons of hell that you are."
> (Matthew 23:15)

If that were not strong enough, Jesus described those guys as "White-washed tombs, who look good on the outside, but are filled with death on the inside" (Matthew 23:27). Clearly, their deep and thorough knowledge of the scriptures held no sway with Jesus. Nor did their lifestyle. In fact, He seemed more opposed to the Pharisees than any other group He encountered. Their problem was not *what* they knew. What they knew was the very Word of God. Their problem was the way they knew it.

THINKING DIFFERENTLY ABOUT THE FALL

While the *word* "sin" is not in the third chapter of Genesis, the *concept* of sin is evidenced throughout. The impact of the Garden event is that Adam and Eve didn't just lose a place to live or lose their status in Creation (although both of those things changed). They literally lost their *way*—their way of seeing and a way of knowing. Their loss, of course, affected the rest of humanity, causing us to inherit a fallen way of seeing. This "sight" impairment makes it difficult for us to understand what really happened that dark day in Eden.

> **"BECAUSE WE SEE ALL THAT WE SEE, WE THINK WHAT WE SEE IS ALL THERE IS."**

For too long we have labored under the perception that Adam and Eve broke a rule and, as a result, sin entered the world. While it is true that Adam and Eve violated God's decree, it is worth re-examining the whole process so that we might see the following things in a new way: 1) our own lives, 2) the life of Jesus (including His death and resurrection), and 3) the intersection between His life and ours.

Prior to the Fall, we have seen that Adam and his bride had a way of seeing and a way of knowing that issued forth directly from the Spirit of God in them. God's Breath came *to* them, resided *in* them, and was broadcast *from* them. This was the plan. This was the way that God operated in and through man so that this couple might bear His image on Earth in the geography they inhabited.

It is crucial that we see this picture. God's Breath came *to* them, resided *in* them, and was broadcast *from* them. We discussed in the last chapter that Jesus came to restore the design of creation. The Breath of God was a significant part of the design that was given up at the Fall and, therefore, a vital piece of the Problem that Jesus came to solve.

As post-Genesis-Chapter-3 people, *what* we think has been shaped by the Fall, but it has also influenced *how* we think. For example, we often labor under the assumption that we should do great things for God. Consider for a moment that God does not want us to do anything for Him. In fact, Acts 17:24-25 makes it clear that God does not need anything from human hands.

It flies in the face of our knowledge of "good" to hear that God does not want us to do anything for Him. Now listen to the contrast: instead, God wants us to do things *from Him*. It has always been God's design that life and all its functions would come from God *to* man and then *through* man into the world. We take dominion over the Creation not by initiating activity, but by first simply receiving a Person. Unless the things that we do, say, and think come first *from God*, the only alternative is that they come from us.

Here is the original design. The Breath of Life comes to us, indwells and empowers us, and flows through us. We represent (think "re-present") God on the Earth, and He accomplishes His plans through us. We must see this design in order to fully grasp what happened the moment that Adam and Eve ate from the Tree of the Knowledge of Good and Evil.

THE DAY IT ALL CHANGED

That day in Eden, Adam and Eve did not just commit an act, they changed a fundamental condition. They changed the flow and state of all I have just described. When they ceased to live by the Breath, they lost a way of knowing. When they consumed the fruit of the Knowledge of Good and Evil, they replaced the Old and Living Way, with a new and insufficient way.

When Adam and Eve took the fruit from the Tree of the Knowledge of Good and Evil into their being, they disconnected themselves (and all of us) from the Source. The Tree of Life, the Spirit of Life, had been their source and their *way* of all things. Disconnecting from this Source didn't just change them from immortal beings to mortals; it left them in a deadly condition.

They disconnected from Life and connected to knowledge. Another way to say this is that they disconnected from God as Source and re-connected to themselves as source. They replaced the flow of Life coming from God with knowledge—their own knowledge. This included not just their knowledge of evil, but also their knowledge of good. Knowledge is not inherently good or evil; it simply *is not Life!*

Their new source—their new way of knowing—distorted and informed their every perception and process and, as a result, ours as well. Their new source became the knowledge of good and knowledge of evil. Sadly, knowledge became their way of searching for what they had lost. Another way to explain what happened is to say that Adam became his own source. Instead of God flowing to him and through him, Adam placed his trust in a new source—his own knowledge and (newly limited) perceptions.

The problem is not simply the knowledge of evil. The problem is that knowledge, in and of itself, can never produce life. Our connection to the new source (the knowledge of good and evil) left us searching for life, the thing we had lost. But we search using our knowledge—a means that can never produce life. Like plugging a data cable into the power port of a computer, no *amount* of data, or any *type* of data, can ever produce power. Similarly, no amount of knowledge and no type of knowledge can ever produce life.

Here is the result. We have come to believe that the proper use of the human will is to choose between good things and evil things. We think the goal is to choose to do good and to avoid bad. Because of the very problem that Jesus came to solve, this actually sounds right to us. To suggest anything else sounds like heresy. But let me suggest something else *anyway*.

DISCONNECT AND RECONNECT

When we rely on our own knowledge to avoid evil and do good, it actually leads us into the dead-end trap of legalism. Like the Pharisees, we will impose our own interpretation of God's rules and totally miss the intent of His heart. The Pharisees regularly tried to catch Jesus in sin by using their knowledge of good. If He healed or dared to pick wheat on the Sabbath, they immediately applied their knowledge of good to prove that Jesus (the Source of all knowledge!) was doing wrong.

Our knowledge of good and evil is not sufficient to reproduce the Life of God on the Earth. Our attempt to operate according to the limitations of human knowledge can actually lead us to *oppose* the Life of God in operation—and we believe we are helping God when we do it!

We have come to believe that Christianity (and therefore discipleship) means getting people off of the "branch" of the knowledge of evil and getting them onto the "branch" of the knowledge of good. Of course, everyone thinks that their own knowledge of good is the correct knowledge of good.

Let's consider the alternative to using our will to avoid evil and engage good. The proper use of the human will is submission to the Spirit of God.

This is different from making a decision to obey or a decision to choose good. It means surrender of control. Here is a fundamental definition of submission: the act of the human will whereby we allow God's power to operate through us instead of exerting our will power from our own knowledge. Electronic appliances submit to electricity on a regular basis. They do not initiate the operation, they surrender to a flow of power instead. When you use your will to try to obey, you are merely trying to resist or control an appetite. However, when you use your will to surrender, God can actually change your appetite.

Here's another way to say it: the proper use of the human will is to decide who will be my source at any given moment. Jesus came to give us access again to the Source of Life, the Source of Power. Now listen to the way many people read John 10:10:

> **"THE PROBLEM IS NOT SIMPLY THE KNOWLEDGE OF EVIL. THE PROBLEM IS THAT KNOWLEDGE, IN AND OF ITSELF, CAN NEVER PRODUCE LIFE."**

> *"The thief comes to steal, to kill and to destroy; but I came that you might behave really, really well until I get back."*

Again, stated this way, we can begin to see how we have thought about the problem Jesus came to solve in knowledge-based or incomplete ways. Here are His actual words:

> *"The thief comes only to steal and kill and destroy; I came that they may have **life**, and have it **abundantly**."* (John 10:10)

Jesus came to reverse the process that we see in Genesis 3. Adam and Eve disconnected from Life and connected to self. Jesus came to give people an opportunity to disconnect from self and reconnect to Life. He did not come to give advice about life, but He came to give a free-flowing infusion of power, flowing from God Himself.

WHY THIS SCARES PEOPLE

When many people hear this message about abandoning the Tree of the

Knowledge of Good and Evil once and for all, a common thought pops into their minds. They immediately think (whether consciously or unconsciously), "But wait! How are we going to keep people from sinning?" The assumption is that we need that fruit in order to inform "good" choices and that we need the fear of punishment to keep us in line.

This is a revealing "Knowledge of Good and Evil" sort of thought. As I said earlier, the word "sin" is not present in Genesis 3, but the *concept* of sin is present throughout. It is this very concept that has been so colored by our knowledge of good and evil. So, let me answer the question, "Who or what will keep people from sinning if we're not operating in the realm of good and evil knowledge?"

I'll answer with a series of questions of my own: What human, freshly filled with the Living Breath of God, is going to rob a bank? What human, connected to, filled by and broadcasting the Spirit of God Himself, is going to look at porn, scream at her kids, covet, commit adultery, or purposefully lie? The answer, of course, is that they would not.

Our dilemma is that we think of sin as behavior that must be managed or controlled. But that thought only makes sense in the context of operating under the Knowledge of Good and Evil. Life is reduced to nothing more than bad behavior avoidance.

> "ADAM AND EVE DISCONNECTED FROM LIFE AND CONNECTED TO SELF. JESUS CAME TO GIVE PEOPLE AN OPPORTUNITY TO DISCONNECT FROM SELF AND RECONNECT TO LIFE."

Just for a moment, reverse the question: what human, filled with the Breath of God, is likely to cure cancer? What man or woman, filled with His Spirit, is likely to do good and bring peace and healing to the world around him? Any human operating under this condition will bring the very presence and operation of God to the spheres that he inhabits. Not only will he *not* "behave badly," but he *will* fill the Earth with the very nature of God.

The shift Jesus came to initiate was our turning our backs on *both* branches of the Tree of Death—the Knowledge of Evil and the Knowledge of Good—and return again to the Tree of Life, where God is our source and He is our Way.

On that fateful day when Adam consumed the forbidden fruit, sin did enter the human race ... but not in the way we usually assume. When Adam neglected the Tree of Life and instead connected to the Tree of the Knowledge of Good and Evil, his condition changed. He was emptied of all that had made him who he had been. In the place inside, where God had been the operating power, there was nothingness.

Adam had to become his own source; and the principle tool for doing so was *knowledge*.

This condition is the problem Jesus came to solve. It's called sin. Man, who was made to contain and broadcast God, was empty and could only broadcast himself. Sin is a condition long before it is a behavior. The condition is emptiness and self-sourced-ness (not a real word, but it should be!).

Sinful behavior is what men and women do in response to the feeling or experience of emptiness. Wrong choices are a direct product of trying to live connected to nothing but self. This is the hook: we too often think of sin as bad behavior that must be replaced by good behavior. But the real answer is much more transformative. Sin is death, and it needs to be replaced with life. While many people fill their emptiness with drugs, sex, and rock and roll, just as many (or more) fill it with performance, perfectionism, or (gasp) even *ministry*.

Both branches of the Tree of Knowledge will kill you. We must walk away from that tree altogether. As we do, we find that the offer from Jesus has always been the same:

> *In Him is* **life** *and that life is the light of men.* (John 1:4)

> *If you knew who I was you would ask, and I would give you rivers of* **Living Water**. (John 4:10)

> *The thief came to steal to kill and to destroy but I came that you might have* **life** *and* **life** *abundantly.* (John 10:10)

Jesus offered Life at every turn—always and only. The offer has ever been this and this alone: to restore mankind to the Tree of Life, because this is what will reverse the collapse in the Garden of Eden.

Jesus—the Way, the Truth, and the Life.

"THE GAME"
A PARABLE—
PART IV

Those who had played The Game that very first day were never the same again. Not only had it changed them, but from that day onward they became *players*. By necessity those who played The Game stayed close to those who played The Game. It took at least eight and preferably twelve people to play. As The Game grew, those who played learned to find one another from one town to the next.

No great advertising campaign was needed. In the same way that a basketball player knows how to find a game, these men and women spotted each other on the way to local fields and parks.

Some were skilled, others were clearly new at The Game, but part of the beauty of a Game that teaches itself is that this distinction simply drew them all together. By nature of The Game, the Veterans embraced and mentored the newer players.

Passers-by were naturally drawn to the sheer joy of The Game, and were invited in to learn. The Game itself had the ability to draw a crowd and was so inviting that anyone who watched was drawn to play.

Some chose to play. Some did not.

CHAPTER 5

PEOPLE OF THE WAY

"Faith minus vulnerability and mystery equals extremism. Or worse, politics."
—Brené Brown

"I've been thinking 'bout the meaning of resistance, of a hope beyond my own. And suddenly the infinite and penitent begin to look like home."
—Switchfoot, Stars

We stood in a tight circle, all heads bowed in the universal "we are praying now" posture. This was a gathering of Christian leaders and it was the man to my immediate left, rather than God, on my mind. The problem was, I knew things about him that he would never have guessed I knew. At that time I worked in private practice as a professional counselor. And one of his victims had confided in me during a confidential session.

Racing through my mind were the same thoughts you would have were you to find yourself standing a few feet from someone who had deeply injured the soul of a loved one: thoughts of vigilante justice—or of something a little less messy, like laying his secret sins bare before this gathering of his peers.

Then he started to pray. The levels of indignation and judgment I was feeling toward him only rose as he delivered the most eloquent prayer I have ever heard. He prayed like a professional orator, his tone commanding attention and his words flowing with poetic turns and emotional expression.

Inside, I was seething and picking apart every hypocrisy-laden utterance.

Think Differently Lead Differently

That's when the Lord spoke to me—a gentle tap on the shoulder interrupting my festival of offendedness. The message was simple and straight to the point. I heard a still, small voice in my mind say, "Hey Bob, at least *he* is praying"—the clear implication being that I was *not*. At that moment, I was in the middle of betraying everything I ever teach regarding forgiveness and the negative power of judgments. In that moment I could not have been any less like Jesus.

My "knowledge of evil" was dictating my thoughts and all my inward responses. Those responses were taking dominion over me, instead of the other way around. The message of that classic bumper sticker about Christians not being perfect, just forgiven, was precisely what I needed at that moment. Clearly *my* imperfections were showing.

Up to this point, we have examined what the life, death, and resurrection of Jesus might mean for the Church as a whole. But what does it all mean for individuals ... for you and me? Most of us desire to live the life God has called us to live and are doing our best to do so. Nevertheless we often still feel as though something is missing. If Jesus has come to set us free and open the veil to another realm—if He has solved the problem of the empty souls of humanity—then how should that impact us? In the words of the late Francis Schaeffer, "How should we then live?"

> **"WE OFTEN TEACH PEOPLE WHAT THEY NEED TO KNOW, BUT WE SELDOM TELL THEM HOW THEY NEED TO KNOW. WE GIVE CONTENT NOT PROCESS."**

In Acts 9:2, we learn that the very first believers were not only called "Christians," they were frequently referred to as belonging to "the Way." I love that. It tracks perfectly with the truth we examined in Chapter Four. Namely, that in the Fall, Adam and Eve lost far more than immortality and access to the garden. They lost a *way*.

It is only appropriate and symmetrical therefore that in His wondrous work of restoration, Jesus enabled us, His followers, to become known as "People of the Way."

I love this also because it is far more than a mere label to stick on people. It's a description of a life process. As we saw in the last chapter, we often teach people *what* they need to know, but we seldom tell them *how* they need to know. We give content not process. Sadly, our movement has been led largely by well-meaning people focused upon telling people *what* to do when it is discovering a *way* that really changes people.

We can see this truth in action in our own homes. Parents often compel a child to apologize to a sibling before the offender has experienced even a hint of remorse about the conflict. "Say you're sorry" is the command. When the "what" (the apology) is the focus of conflict resolution instead of the "way" (heartfelt regret), then the child's coerced "I'm sorry" can ring with resentment. The difference is in the *way* through which the words arrived. And what a difference!

In a similar way, Christian leaders so often focus on what to do, instead of how to be. In the next few pages, we'll examine some of the fundamental elements of the Christian way in this new light. And we'll begin with the very concept of Salvation itself.

YOU MUST BE BORN AGAIN

Years ago, in a meeting of about 100 pastors, we had an intense discussion about the nature of salvation. Before the meeting ended, three of those veteran Christian leaders received the New Birth for the first time in their lives. I have learned to never assume that this issue is settled in the life of a person simply because he or she has spent many years attending church (or even leading one). Frankly, many church-goers are confused about this issue. And this confusion is passed along from generation to spiritual generation.

We must settle that the salvation of a soul is a work of God, not man. Why is this distinction so important? Because if you listen to the language that many people use when praying to be saved, or when describing their experience, it often focuses on *their* activity instead of the free gift God has provided for them.

The typical vocabulary of salvation is laden with personal pronouns and action verbs: "I *commit* to *follow* Jesus. I give Him everything I have." These phrases are commonly used as a model for leading others to a saving knowledge of Jesus; but such wording focuses on something that the person can do. A man can commit to follow a politician or a teacher. A woman can give everything to the IRS. These are human acts. Doing those same human acts in relation to God does not produce the New Birth.

Recall the language the Savior Himself used as He described his mission at Zaccheus' house:

> *And Jesus said to him, "Today salvation has come to this house ... For the Son of Man has come to seek and to save that which was lost."* (Luke 19:10)

Here, all the action verbs reside on Jesus' side of the ledger. Salvation *comes* ... the Son of man seeks and *saves*. Notice the same thing in the two verses that immediately follow Romans 8:28, one of the most memorized and often quoted verses in all the Bible:

> *For those whom He **foreknew**, He also **predestined** to become **conformed** to the image of His Son, so that He would be the firstborn among many brethren; and these whom He **predestined**, He also **called**; and these whom He **called**, He also **justified**; and these whom He **justified**, He also **glorified**.* (Romans 8:29-30)

Again, these verses are filled with action and doing, but it is God engaged in all the acting and doing. That being said, there are two things every person who receives salvation does. We find both in this classic biblical passage on the New Birth:

> *"THE WORD IS NEAR YOU, IN YOUR MOUTH AND **IN YOUR HEART**"—that is, the word of faith which we are preaching, that if you confess with your mouth Jesus as Lord, and **believe in your heart** that God raised Him from the dead, you shall be saved; for **with the heart man believes**, resulting in righteousness, and with the mouth he confesses, resulting in salvation. For the Scripture says, "WHOEVER BELIEVES IN HIM WILL NOT BE DISAPPOINTED."* (Romans 10:8-11)

To be saved we must "believe." The only other necessary thing on our part is to confess Jesus as Lord. Not just repeat the phrase when coached, but genuinely confess Him as Lord. Lest this become confusing, let me be clear and direct. Confessing Jesus as Lord is not an act. It is more accurate to say it is ceasing an act. Let me illustrate.

One day I was talking with a husband and wife who were in a very difficult situation. In the course of the conversation it became evident that neither of these individuals had ever been born again. Both agreed that they wanted to pray to be saved. I helped them by suggesting words for them to pray. When the prayer was over, both looked up. She looked like the weight of the world had been lifted from her shoulders. He looked at her, then at me, then back at her again, then tried to get his face to look like hers. They had uttered the same words, but the long-term effects of those words were starkly different.

Months later, her life was transformed. His life, however, had gone from bad to worse. He came alone to see me.

"That thing didn't work," he said.

"What thing?" I knew what he meant.

"That prayer we prayed a few months ago, it didn't work." His frustration was evident.

"Well, let me tell you my experience that day, sitting across from the two of you," I told him, and began to describe to him the scene I just described above.

"Let me tell you what I think I saw that day," I continued as he grunted permission. "Your wife surrendered her heart freely that day. You said the same words she did, but you seemed to be trying to do whatever you needed to get her off your back. Would you agree?" I asked.

Grudgingly, he began to nod.

"The key here is surrender, not magic words. The position of your heart matters far more than the language on your lips. Would you like to surrender today?" I asked.

My story would be better if he had answered *yes*. But he didn't. Sadly, his response is common. He chose not to surrender. It is much easier to follow a prescription than to actually surrender control, and receiving Jesus as Lord is exactly that. It is not an act; it is *ceasing* to act. It means giving up on trying to be your own source and your own foundation. It means you abandon the prideful, futile effort of trying to generate your own strength, rely upon your own ideas, and cling to your own ways of knowing. When a person finally surrenders, Jesus takes over. God waits for us to surrender—to finally come to the end of ourselves—so He can take action on our behalf.

When a man or woman is born again, it is not simply a change of eternal destination. The New Birth brings people into a new life, gives them a new nature, a connection to a new source, and the capacity to see and live in a (previously) invisible realm. In other words, they receive a new Way.

Let's look at some crucial characteristics of these "People of the Way."

THE HIDDEN HEART REVEALED

People of the Way live unguarded and unbearable lives.

Since my first day in the family of God, I have carried a picture of Jesus in my mind. I see Him as a man of unflinching eye contact and unguarded affection. I see Him as infinitely secure, without any self-comparison to others. I see Him as a man with no hidden-ness, so that what is in His deepest core is plainly expressed through His words, His face, and His posture.

In the eighth chapter of John, Jesus promises that if we abide in His word, we can know the truth and the truth will set us free. In using the term "truth," I don't believe Jesus was referring merely to accurate information. I believe He was talking about authenticity, integrity and congruence. Indeed, the Greek word translated "truth" in John 8:32, *alétheia*, carries clear connotations of "sincerity" and "reality."

If what is on the inside does not match what is on the outside, it does not matter how thorough and accurate your doctrine is, nor how clearly you have it in your mind. Consider this: informational truth that is not congruent with experiential truth is not yet complete truth. To confirm this point, let's examine a startling set of verses in an earlier section of John's gospel:

> *"This is the judgment, that the Light has come into the world, and men loved the darkness rather than the Light, for their deeds were evil. For everyone who does evil hates the Light, and does not come to the Light for fear that his deeds will be exposed. But **he who practices the truth comes to the Light**, so that his deeds may be manifested as having been wrought in God."* (John 3:19-21)

I characterized that passage as "startling" because it contains an unexpected contrast. We're accustomed to contrasting evil with good. In fact, we reflexively consider the opposite of evil to be *good*. That's to be expected because we've been hanging out in the deep shade of the Tree of Knowledge of Good and Evil for a very long time. Most people would play back the message of the above passage like this: "Everyone who does evil hates the light; but those who practice good, come to the light."

But that is not what Jesus said. Read His words again. He said, "He who practices *the truth* comes to the light." In God's moral economy, the opposite of evil is not *good*. Its opposite is *truth*!

This means no one can generate his or her own goodness. When we bring our own perceptions of the truth into the presence of God, He does an amazing thing. He transforms the evil into something new that now emanates from Him. He takes the emptiness that has been honestly brought before Him and fills it—with Himself. We can bring God our worst, and do so unguarded and without defense. When we allow His light to reveal the truth, our spiritual eyes are opened to see reality from His true perspective instead of our false one. God's truth flowing through us then transforms our hearts, changing us in that particular area to experience and reflect the goodness of God. *Our part is not to manufacture good, but to walk in truth regarding the contents of our hearts.* For example, when we force a smile even though we're grieving, we take from God an opportunity to be the Source of our comfort. When we walk into church on Sunday morning with a heart full of care and pain and then answer the inevitable question ("How are you doing?") with a dishonest "I'm blessed," we deny the Spirit of God residing within our fellow believers the opportunity to work through them.

> **"OUR PART IS NOT TO MANUFACTURE GOOD, BUT TO WALK IN TRUTH REGARDING THE CONTENTS OF OUR HEARTS."**

In contrast, when we come to God with our hearts uncovered, we connect to Him as our Source. We partake of His Life, and transformation is a glorious byproduct. When we come fearlessly into the light, the truth sets us free.

SEEK FIRST THE KINGDOM

People of the Way learn to seek first the Kingdom.

"But seek first the Kingdom and His righteousness and all these things shall be added to you" (Matthew 6:33).

In this brief but brilliant statement, Jesus offers us a picture of reality and a principle to guide every facet of our lives. Leading up to this statement, Jesus had been addressing the things that people worry about. He pointed out the *way* that people live: worried about provision, worried about safety, worried about comfort. Then He drops the bomb.

"Why worry?" He says. "These are things that people without God worry about. But if you will seek the Kingdom of God first (and receive the righteousness I have come to give you, i.e., trust Me as your Source), then *all those things* will be added to you."

C. S. Lewis clearly had this truth in view when he said, "Aim at Heaven and you will get Earth thrown in. Aim at Earth and you get neither." In Matthew

6:33, Jesus is simultaneously painting a picture of reality (as a corrective to the false picture most of us carry around) and prescribing the single most important principle for people of the Way.

First of all, He is telling us that there is a realm within reach, though out of sight. That there is more to life than what we see. He is even implicitly telling us something about the relationship between the two realms: the invisible realm actually supplies and supports the visible realm.

Secondly, He is declaring this stunningly simple, yet life changing principle:

Whatever you seek first organizes every other facet of your life.

"Seeking first" is not simply a matter of chronology. It is about priority. We seek first what we value the most. We seek first anything to which we give our time, our energy, our thoughts and our focus. Everyone alive has something they are seeking first. Whatever that something is, it has power over every other aspect of our lives.

As a counselor and pastor, I have seen first-hand how this priority dynamic robs people of life and joy. It is often the case that by the time a person contacts a counselor the perceived problem has bloomed into a very high priority. In most cases, the issue and its resolution have become the thing they are "seeking first." If they are depressed, they seek first relief from depression. If they are having family conflict,

> **"SEEKING FIRST THE KINGDOM OF GOD WILL ESTABLISH DIVINE ORDER OVER EVERY ASPECT OF OUR LIVES."**

they seek first to find resolution. Whether the issue is anger, addiction, or any other of the myriad human ills, eventually the need for relief from the symptom becomes all consuming. Here's why.

If they "seek first" relief from depression, depression gains control over *every other aspect* of their lives. If they seek first victory over addiction, that addiction gains control. It is the Seek First Principle at work—backfiring on all who misunderstand it.

Jesus wants us to grasp the truth of this principle so we can be victorious *in* it instead of victimized by it. Seeking first the Kingdom of God will establish divine order over every aspect of our lives; therefore, we will have power over depression, anger, addiction, and anything else that tries to control us or disengage us from the Life God has provided.

THE KINGDOM

So what exactly does it mean to "Seek first the Kingdom of God?" If this should be the central pursuit of people of the Way, this question merits some time and attention. We need to understand what we are pursuing and how it is pursued. Often it is not what we think it is, because that darned tree (of the Knowledge of Good and Evil) has colored our thoughts on all things spiritual.

As we've already seen, ever since the Fall our default way of knowing has been centered upon *knowledge* and *doing*—the knowledge (of good and evil) and doing (right things and abstaining from wrong things). In other words, we attempt to build a tower to Heaven on a foundation of our own knowledge, with bricks of good choices held together by the mortar of will power. This human-sourced edifice invariably crumbles.

If this is our way of knowing, here is how we're likely to perceive the words of Matthew 6:33. Let's call this the Knowledge of Good and Evil (mis) translation:

> *"Try hard to do all the things God wants, and to live in all the ways God asks; if you do fairly well at this, He will reward you with the other things you are hoping for."* (KGET)

The Kingdom of God doesn't operate the way human kingdoms do. In Earthly kingdoms, the monarch issues decrees and conveys those edicts to the people. Then the people decide whether or not they will obey. They carry out their lives accordingly—either as law-abiding subjects or outlaw rebels. In every form of human government, someone has authority to make laws and then enforce consequences for those who choose to disobey.

So often (too often), we apply this mindset to God's Kingdom. This is our knowledge of Good and Evil default setting coloring our perception of reality and governing how we think about and therefore relate to God.

However, God's laws and decrees cannot be broken. We can break ourselves against them, but God's laws actually enforce themselves. To best understand this, consider the law of gravity. No one has the option of deciding to obey or disobey gravity. Everyone has the opportunity to decide how to relate to it. But gravity will enforce itself. God does not have to send a sheriff to enforce gravity.

The laws of God's Kingdom are simply a description of reality as God has designed it. People who honor their parents live longer. Consequences happen to those who fling themselves against God's design.

God's Kingdom is like an oven. The reigning force in an oven is heat. Anything that enters it cooks, melts, burns or in some way is changed by the nature of that kingdom. The heat does the work; the cookie dough merely receives. Think about what happens if you put a hot cookie in your mouth. The heat has come *to* the cookie; it has resided *in* the cookie; then the heat is broadcast to your tongue *from* the cookie. Does this sound familiar?

God's Kingdom is actually an expression of all of the elements of Jesus' mission described in the previous chapter. It is God living among men. It is His realm invading ours. When Jesus exhorted us to seek God's Kingdom and "His righteousness," He was referring to the original design or original condition when all things were right. All things were an expression of God's perfect blueprint.

Here's a simple definition: the "Kingdom" is God's nature, knowledge and power *expressed*—now, in our present circumstances. Whenever Jesus stood before a crowd and proclaimed, "The Kingdom of Heaven has come among men," invariably a remarkable expression of God's power and knowledge followed. Crippled legs straightened and gained strength; lepers were made clean; selfish men became generous; the grieving received the ultimate comfort (having their deceased loved ones made alive again). All of these experiences were God's Kingdom operating in the theater of Earth.

Notice that no leg considered its options and then opted to straighten out. No leper's skin chose to obey the rule. Hearts were first aligned with the Kingdom, then legs and skin were affected. Our part is to seek and say yes to the Kingdom—to get in agreement with His willingness, power, and authority as the cleansed leper and the faith-filled Centurion did in Matthew 8:2-13. Our part is to plug in, and His part is to deliver the power.

When Zaccheus' heart was changed, he did not hasten to return money to those he had cheated because Jesus explained a regulation to him. He did it because a new force was propelling his heart and driving his thinking.

The Kingdom is God's power among us to do for us what is impossible for us to do for ourselves. Its principal characteristic is the work of God in us rather than our work *for God*. People moved by the impulse of God's Kingdom ruling in their hearts naturally and un-self-consciously accomplish all manner of wonderful things. In contrast, those who strive to do "good" things out of duty, guilt, compulsion, fear, or pride are not seeking first the Kingdom. They are seeking to assuage or satisfy those things that are driving them. They are self-sourced, not Heaven-sourced. That is why they are so prone to burn out. It's why many despair of ever seeing God's power manifest. Disappointment and frustration are the inevitable result of trying to operate while connected to a powerless source.

Have you ever wondered why an appliance wasn't working—even after you had adjusted all the dials and knobs—and then had someone come along and ask, "Is it plugged in?" As we come to understand what it actually means to seek first the Kingdom, we will see that this is the very question implicit in Jesus' statement. People struggle mightily to bring resolution to every facet of life. They strive and strain to provide for themselves. They make countless adjustments and turn over innumerable new leaves. But with one sentence, Jesus turns our attention to the primary issue: "Is it plugged in?" If you will "plug in" to God as your power Source, you'll be amazed at how those knobs and dials that seemed so ineffective will all begin to function as they should.

A COMMON THREAD

Please notice a theme developing as we explore how to live as people of the Way. In all of the topics covered so far—Salvation, unguardedness, and Kingdom-seeking—we see a common thread. That thread is: God as initiator and man as receiver (more on this in a later chapter).

First, we see that Salvation comes from God to men. It is His power and His initiative that characterizes men and women receiving the New Birth. Second, we see that when we uncover our hearts, and allow Him to keep us in this position, it is His work that changes us, inserting new power into our souls. And finally, regarding the Kingdom of God, we make a shift in focus from what we *should* do for God, to what *only God can do* for us.

The shift is all about becoming people who have a new way. The problem that Jesus came to solve was that mankind had lost its connection to God and, therefore, to a way of being and a way of knowing. Jesus restored to us a new and a Living Way. This Way is characterized not just by new habits, but by a new Source. Habits can be changed by our Knowledge of Good and Evil. But our source can only be changed as we learn the practice of daily surrender; or, stated another way, agreeing that Jesus is Lord.

THE KINGDOM COMES TO US

People of the Way are great receivers.

The Kingdom comes to human beings, it inhabits them, and then it is broadcast through them to the world. I will probably repeat this again, even before the chapter is over, because we must get this ingrained in our thinking. If it does not come *to* us first, then the things we broadcast issue forth from us, not from God.

How does the Kingdom come to us? The answer to this question will define the central practice of "seeking first the Kingdom." The answer to this question will also answer the most common question I am asked: "Now that I am beginning to think differently, what should I *do*?"

The simplest answer I can give to this not-so-simple question is this: Learn to hear God's voice. God's voice was Adam's lifeline in the Garden of Eden. It was God's voice that the entire nation of Israel was invited to hear at the top of the mountain. It was, and always has been, about helping people to become the kind who live by every word that proceeds from His mouth (Deuteronomy 8:3).

God never intended that only a select few would hear His voice and shout it to the masses. That model is a result of humans who prefer to live by the Knowledge of Good and Evil. God knows something about the power of His voice that we too easily forget. God's voice is not simply a sound that carries symbols used to deliver information. God's voice is *the* creative force that brought into existence all that is. When God speaks, He is delivering far more than mere information and concepts. God's voice is the way His power is transferred from one place to another. God is delivering far more than concepts. He is delivering the very reality that His words contain.

When I say the word "peace" it is a suggestion. When God says "peace" it is a substance that transfers actual peace to the hearer. Hearing His voice is the way that we plug back in to His Kingdom. Learning to hear His voice is the number one activity of seeking first His Kingdom.

As my colleague Alan Smith says in his excellent book, *Unveiled: The Transforming Power of God's Presence and Voice*, any model of discipleship that does not turn people to hear God's active voice has no power to transform the disciple. The life Jesus came to give us has always been about individuals being connected to their God. It has always been about the creative power of His Voice and Presence coming *to* us, living *in* us, and working *through* us.

The purpose of my book is not to convince you that God still speaks to people today, nor is it designed to tell you how to hear and discern God's voice. But it is impossible to connect some of the main points I want to convey without first acknowledging this truth: one of the central activities of people of the Way is to hear the voice of God, and to pursue hearing the voice of God.

FAITH

People of the Way learn to obtain faith by hearing the voice of God.

Not only is hearing God's voice the central activity in the life of the Way, it is the source of this thing that we call faith.

> *"So faith comes from hearing and hearing by the Word of Christ."* (Romans 10:17)

This is one more crucial aspect of our walk with God that comes from Him and not from us. So often we think that faith is something that we must work up in order to please God. We push our thoughts, psych ourselves up and out, striving to raise our level of thinking and believing. But all this effort just reveals that we still think we are the source of faith.

The above verse makes it quite clear that God is the source of faith. Our role should not be surprising. We choose to listen to Him instead of other voices. Faith is simply the result of hearing what God has said and is saying to us. This is the all-important first step. Faith, the book of Hebrews tells us, is the substance of things not seen (11:1). Faith connects us to the invisible realm and converts the unseen words of God in the spiritual realm into something that can be witnessed in the visible realm. Faith (believing God) comes by hearing, and hearing (developing the sensitivity and capacity of your spiritual ears to hear God's voice) comes a certain *way*—by The Word—Jesus. His words fine-tune our spiritual ears to recognize the voice of God.

How can we know this is true? Because Jesus said, *"I only say whatever I hear the Father saying"* (John 12:49,50). So if we want to recognize the kind of things God says, we need to listen to whatever Jesus says. Hearing fulfills the mission of Jesus in our souls. Jesus came to show us the Father. And the Father said, *"This is my beloved Son, in whom I am well pleased; hear Him"* (Matthew 17:5).

If you feel you are having trouble hearing God, fill your heart with the words of Jesus. And your spiritual ears will become sensitive to the vocabulary of God—the *way* He speaks. People of the Way are connected to Jesus, the Way (*"I am **the way**, the truth and the life"*). He is the One who reveals the way God speaks.

AUTHORITY

When we are given authority for Kingdom purposes, we must come to understand that God gives authority for specific reasons, and with a specific function in mind. A leader can either use their authority to serve themselves, or to serve others. One will ultimately result in loss of authority and the other will result in increase.

We must examine how God Himself uses authority, to really understand the reasons or functions for which He grants authority to individuals.

Jesus, who surrenders to the Father and lowers Himself to the form of a servant (Philippians 2) is then exalted, or lifted up by His Father. God uses His authority in this case to lift up the one who has chosen to relinquish His authority.

When Jesus, who is the head of the Church, exercises His position of authority, He grants the church His authority and lifts it up. Again and again we see that God Himself uses His authority to lift up and empower those who are weak. God-given authority is to grant authority and opportunity to those who do not have it.

Like any resource that we have, where we choose to invest determines the yield that the investment will return. Invest your authority in protecting and providing for the weak, God will grant more. Invest your authority in making your life or circumstances easier, and God is much less likely to increase your authority.

Spiritual authority is more than simply selfless; it is generous to the weak.

WALKING IN THE WAY

I know I have thrown a lot of potentially paradigm rattling stuff at you over the last dozen or so pages. So, allow me to summarize by getting very practical and specific about what I'm suggesting we've been missing—both as individual believers and as leaders who disciple others.

I'm convinced there are two traits that characterize people who live gloriously, freely, fruitfully in the Way.

The first characteristic of a person of the Way is *vulnerability*. This is that raw honesty before God that I mentioned previously in the section labeled "The Hidden Heart Revealed." Your heart is soft. Your soul is uncovered in front of God and men. Oh, what freedom and simplicity are found in living this way! Frankly, it's a lot of work walking around covered up—pretending to the world we are somebody we are not. I've tried to live that way. It's exhausting. Yet that is precisely how most believers live their lives. Why? Shame and fear—the result of eating of the Tree of the Knowledge of Good and Evil—keeps us doing it. And frankly, we've made our churches the last place anyone is likely to feel it safe to drop the "I have it all together!" pretense.

What if you're struggling? What if you're weak? What if you're afraid? What if things are falling apart? Can you be honest with some people about that? Can people be honest with you about that?

These are vital questions because without vulnerability our connection to God is limited or even blocked altogether. And yet fearless vulnerability is one of the rarest things on Earth. The original people of the Way had to trust Jesus enough to become like children so that they could approach Him with the kind of hearts that would understand when He talked about leaven, He wasn't taking a stand against bread. They had to approach Him with hearts that were open enough to say, "We really don't get it. We just know we trust you."

Little children don't know how to do the whole false-fronted pretense thing. You know exactly how they're feeling. This childlike vulnerability is the first of the two traits that mark people who walk in the Way. The second (and most important) trait is also found in abundance in little ones.

People of the Way are great receivers. To understand why this is so vital, you have to recall that the very nature and function of the Kingdom of God is that we receive, contain and broadcast things from the invisible Heavenly realm to the natural, visible realm. You and I cannot broadcast what we do not contain. And we can't contain what we won't receive. Do you see it? In order for us to do anything born of God's creative intention, we must first receive it from Him.

This is why I can confidently make a statement that in many religious quarters sounds outrageous ... heretical even. That is, God is never going to ask you to do anything *for* Him. His design is that we do everything *from* Him. Anything you attempt to do *for* Him initiates from you. It is self-sourced rather than God-sourced, and that type of doing was never His original purpose. Self-sourced doing is powerless to express God in this world.

This is why being vulnerable, openhearted and receptive are *the* keys to this Way of living. If this is true, and I believe with all my heart it is, then we are faced with some uncomfortable but vitally important questions:

How can we as church leaders transform our churches into places that point people to the Way? How can the cultures and communities we influence be influenced to become places that receive, contain and broadcast the Life of God? By now you won't be surprised to learn I have some thoughts about those questions.

Onward.

A PARABLE— PART V

Those who had watched but not played had been a part of the History as well. Just not the part that they thought.

Clear as it was that they were watching something important, they were never quite sure exactly what they were seeing. But human nature would never tolerate such confusion. Sure or not, they developed a certain sure-ness about what they did know.

Two primary groups developed from this crowd of spectators. The group that had eventually produced the Master Teachers had taken it upon themselves to write down all the rules and what they could learn from observing strategy. The application of the rules, of course, led to knowing how to play.

The second group was the more vocal, energetic group. Bent toward engagement and a less cognitive response, this group developed a way to encourage players and non-players alike. Cheers, songs, and even large events like a high school pep rally grew out of the overflow of excitement this group had experienced on that first day.

These groups became well organized over time, and found ways to draw people to their gatherings. By function one group was a bit headier and more cognitive, and the other group more gregarious. However, neither offered the actual experience of playing The Game, so over time they had to develop and rely on strategies to continue to draw people to their gatherings.

Organizations grew and structured around these two groups, and building and maintaining these organizations became a part of their function as well.

Often it seemed there was even some confusion between these gatherings and The Game itself. When people were looking to learn and play they could actually be steered to one of these meetings inadvertently.

If they did not know better, they could walk into one of these groups and think they were actually learning The Game. Even some of the organizers grew confused about this line. What they were doing was important, and it pointed people toward The Game. Perhaps they actually were an extension of The Game.

CHAPTER 6

WHO'S THE PRESIDENT OF BASKETBALL?

"Take me to your leader."
—Marvin the Martian

"If our culture is to be transformed, it will happen from the bottom up—from ordinary believers practicing apologetics over the backyard fence or around the barbecue grill."
—Chuck Colson

The binary title of this book is mirrored by its two-part structure. In the chapters up to this point, we have laid the groundwork by exploring the "Think Differently" half of this equation. Now, having wandered in the wilderness for six chapters having our paradigms shaken and assumptions challenged, it's time to cross the Jordan and enter the "Lead Differently" land of promise. Are you ready?

I've pointed out the pitfalls of changing the wrong thing and affecting change at the wrong level—tinkering with content rather than adopting a new process. I've asked us to think differently about the problem Jesus came to solve—disconnectedness and self-sourced-ness rather than Sin. I've challenged us to think differently about the mission of Jesus—giving us a Way, not a What.

The next question I want to explore is how we as pastors and leaders can apply these insights to the challenges of leading people and transforming this thing we call the church (universal and local).

At first blush it might seem odd that a book about Kingdom leadership would devote so much initial space to establishing fundamental assumptions and underlying presuppositions. But my concern has been that if we're trying to lead the wrong thing we're certainly going to lead in wrong ways. We can't afford to be like our medieval cat-killing forebears.

The same is true when it comes to defining the local church. Is every place that slaps the word "church" on a shingle really a church? For example, there is an extended family group from Kansas that seems to get itself in the news with astonishing regularity. They call themselves "Westboro Baptist Church." The charming little group is seemingly never in Westboro, is not affiliated with any Baptist denomination, and is not a church in any commonly understood meaning of the term. Other than that I suppose it's the perfect name.

In all seriousness, this clan displays the word *church* in their name and yet wherever they go they only spit hatred and venom at any group that violates their acutely attuned knowledge of good and evil. And they proclaim to the world, "We are the Church." At other points along the "church" continuum we find people with a wild array of beliefs, values, worship modes, discipleship methodologies, and perceptions of mission—all proudly flying the banner of "church."

As you may have discerned by now, I like to use stories and questions as aids to understanding. So, allow me to pose a question. I must warn you in advance that the question may at first blush seem silly. The fact is, it often takes a silly question to expose a silly way of thinking. Here's the question:

Who is the president of basketball?

I warned you. But let's explore this question for a moment. The way you would try to respond to this query is a direct reflection of where your mind goes when you hear the term "basketball." For example, when confronted with the question, "Who is the president of basketball?" many people's minds will by default go to the National Basketball Association—the professional basketball league in the United States. The NBA does indeed have a president who's a fairly well known figure among those who follow sports.

But that presents another question: Is the NBA all there is of "basketball"? What about college hoops? There are a variety of divisions within NCAA basketball depending upon school size—and each division has its own president. People associated with such divisions might answer the question, "Who is the president of basketball?" in very different ways. But wait ...

what about the tens of thousands of city and county recreational leagues proliferating throughout the country? What about other countries? Basketball is gaining popularity everywhere. It's a global phenomenon.

The question, "Who is the president of basketball?" forces us to think about what we mean by *basketball*. Here is my point. Basketball can be anything from an NBA event where The Game is played before live audiences of ten thousands and television audiences of millions by highly skilled professionals earning millions of dollars, to two poor kids in a park with a net-less iron hoop and a tattered, under-inflated basketball. Both activities and everything in between are fully legitimate expressions of *basketball*. Indeed the variety of possible legitimate expressions is almost infinite.

The real question I'm setting up is this: Who is the president of this global phenomenon called *church*? Who's the head of church?

Of course there are two perspectives from which to view that question. The first is from Earth looking up, and the other is from Heaven looking down. Certainly, the standard Sunday School quiz answer to that question is that Jesus is the head of the Church. And the Bible, speaking from the Heavenly vantage point, is unequivocal in its declaration of Jesus' headship over the Church. But is that how we run our local churches? It seems to me that from our Earthbound vantage point, we tend to think more along one of these lines:

- The pastor is the head of the church.
- The governing body is the head of the church.
- The denominational headquarters is the head of the church.

We think this way because we have tended to view only traditional forms and manifestations of the local church as truly *church*. But what about three guys sitting around the table somewhere with utterly no signs of organization or hierarchy—but all three of them contain the Spirit of God? What if these three believers are honoring Jesus with what they're doing and saying, and together they are engaging His presence and truth in ways that transform their inner man? Is that "church?"

As you might suspect, my answer is, "Yes!" Just as three kids in a driveway can be playing basketball, three guys around the table somewhere can be having church. With all that in mind, there is a question I want to explore. We know that Jesus came to Earth, lived in relative obscurity for roughly thirty years, engaged in public ministry for three years, then died, rose and ascended to Heaven where He took His royal seat at the right hand of the Father. The question is, what did He intend to leave behind?

The fact is, if we examine what the New Testament records of Jesus' entire ministry front to end, we find that He rarely talked about the "church" (*ecclesia*), but spoke frequently about the "kingdom" (*basileia*) and consistently talked about people—where they were and what they needed in the moment. He was all about bringing the Kingdom and the people together.

FATHERLESS WHEAT

The "church"—universal and local—is a difficult thing to define. Keep in mind that *leading differently* is where we're headed on this journey. One of the parables of Jesus is particularly instructive in this regard.

In an effort to communicate a truth, Jesus once told a story about a certain man who owned a wheat field in which he had recently sown wheat seeds (Matthew 13). But in the middle of the night an enemy came along and sowed tare seeds among all the wheat. As both types of plant began to emerge from the Earth, a farmhand came to the field's owner with the distressing news and asked him if he wanted them to start ripping up the tares. The landowner's response was:

> *"No; for while you are gathering up the tares, you may uproot the wheat with them. Allow both to grow together until the harvest; and in the time of the harvest I will say to the reapers, 'First gather up the tares and bind them in bundles to burn them up; but gather the wheat into my barn.'"* (v. 29-30)

For most of my life as a Christian I have heard this parable interpreted as being about good people and evil people in the world. I have even taught some version of that interpretation in the past. But in recent years I have come to a different understanding of what Jesus was communicating. To be specific, I think the master's "field" is the Church.

First, please note that the Master owns this field. It belongs to Him, just as the Church belongs to Christ. Note also that He has things growing in there—things He intentionally planted. I think it's revealing that Paul once described the church in Corinth collectively as "God's field":

> *For we are God's fellow workers; you are God's field, God's building.* (I Corinthians 3:9)

Finally, note that an outlaw "enemy" slipped into that field and planted other things—tares—that emerged right there among the things the Master planted.

According to an authoritative reference source, a "tare" is actually a bastardized form of wheat. In other words, it is a fatherless form of wheat—a mutated plant that has half of the DNA of wheat and half from another plant. The result is a plant that looks very much like wheat, particularly in the early stages of growth, but when mature has no capacity to bear fruit. Nothing edible or nutritious results—in fact, they are toxic if ingested.

This is why, in the parable, the two types of plants will be easily distinguished at harvest time.

Now if, as I believe, Jesus is trying to teach us something about the church here, precisely what is the lesson? Well, imagine that you and I are part of a local congregation of believers and that our mutual church home is metaphorically a wheat field. You and I would be wheat plants growing in that field precisely where the Master planted us as seeds (or "fathered" us). However, we might look around and see others who look just like we do—but upon closer inspection we might perceive that they are fatherless. And by *fatherless* I don't mean they don't have a human origin point. I mean that they have not yet been born again. Or put in the terms of the previous chapter, they have not yet become People of the Way. They are *tares*.

I think most mainstream Christians would agree that one definition of the Church is "a corporate gathering of those who have received the New Birth." That may indeed be an accurate definition, but is it a complete one? I don't think there's a single senior pastor that would look around and say that every single person in his congregation is born again, but the sign on the side of the building still carries the word "church."

It's a conundrum. If a church by definition is made up of believers, how can there be unbelievers in a church?

OUR IDENTITY CRISIS

Widespread fuzzy thinking about this very issue is a key part of my motivation for writing this book. Indeed, I believe that the Church itself is experiencing something of an identity crisis. Even in our own midst *we* are not always *us*—meaning every wheat field contains both wheat and tares.

Let's back up and talk about why this is such a challenge for us, and why it's important to address it biblically and clearly.

Some say the authentic "church" is comprised of people who really know and value the Word of God. Some say it's comprised of people of faith. But others say, "Wait, faith without works is dead. So, the real-deal church is characterized by people who go out into the world and do the stuff." Still others focus on getting everyone's doctrine straightened out—thinking that if we can all become good, sound, Reformed or Charismatic or Dispensational or Whatever—then we'll *really* be the Church. In reality, all of these viewpoints are looking to define the Church in terms of what its people *do* rather than who their Source is.

Part of the problem is that, try as we might, we can never capture the one *thing* that is *the* thing we all must do or believe to be the Church. All the while, the only thing that truly makes us the Church is having been fathered by the right Source. The Church is the corporate gathering of the People of the Way—people who contain the presence of God because they are born *of* Him and connected *to* Him. The Church is the agency in the world that brings God's presence back to the planet, just as foreseen by the prophet Habakkuk:

> **"PART OF THE PROBLEM IS THAT, TRY AS WE MIGHT, WE CAN NEVER CAPTURE THE ONE THING THAT IS THE THING WE ALL MUST DO OR BELIEVE TO BE THE CHURCH."**

For the Earth will be filled with the knowledge of the glory of the Lord, as the waters cover the sea. (Habakkuk 2:14)

God's mission statement is to cover the Earth with His nature, and His strategy is you and me. By the way, the Hebrew word translated "knowledge" in the verse above is completely unrelated to the Hebrew word that appears in the Genesis phrase "tree of the *knowledge* of good and evil." The word in this passage from Habakkuk speaks of awareness—of perception. In other words, through the God-connected, God-sourced presence of People of the Way, the whole world will eventually come to perceive the glory of God.

Once again, we've got to understand that mere *doing* is not what makes people the People of the Way—even though People of the Way do lots of things. It is the Source of their doings that distinguishes them.

We see a foretaste of this reality in Old Testament Israel. What ultimately defined Israel as a "people" was God's Presence—His glory—among them. Likewise, a tangible, identifiable, fragrance of Christ's essence characterized the first believers: "*Now as they observed the confidence of Peter and John and understood that they were uneducated and untrained men, they were amazed, and began to recognize them as having been with Jesus"* (Acts 4:13).

When we as leaders fall into the trap of defining the church in terms of what people do, we unavoidably end up focusing on "first order" issues (hopefully you recall our levels of change discussion in Chapter Three.)

For decades we've ridden the swinging pendulum from one type of first order change to the other. For example, huge debates roil Christendom about whether we should be leading people in the direction of being more doctrinal, or more "missional," or more something-else-altogether.

Please don't get me wrong. I'm a Word of God guy. I believe the Bible is a miraculous, inerrant revelation of God's character and will. Doctrine matters. But as we observed back in Chapter Four, the Pharisees were the ultimate Word of God guys. But their deeply held ways of knowing made them purveyors of death rather than God's life. Nevertheless, in the last half of the last century we led wave after wave of first order change in which leaders worked feverishly to get everyone's theology straightened out (of course there were scores of versions of what "right" theology looked like). The thought was, "Hey guys, if we do not believe the right things about (pick your poison: eschatology, God's sovereignty, the scope of the Atonement, the place and role of the Holy Spirit), then we're not being the Church!"

Now the pendulum seems to have careened off in another direction. A generation of leaders looks at the "doctrine" guys of the past and says, "Hey, faith without works is dead. It's what we *do* with what we've seen in the Word that matters. The Church has got to be this missional organization, and if the Church isn't missional then it's not really being the Church!"

"Learn the Word!"

"No, heal the World!"

Of course, these two sets of marching orders are not necessarily mutually exclusive. And there is much about the missional message that I find appealing and resonate.

I have an uncle who, ever since Hurricane Katrina devastated New Orleans in 2005, has made an annual trip down to South Louisiana. He throws his tools in the back of his truck, grabs some like-minded Christian friends, and they head south to build, repair and restore. No Bible studies. No worship services. No tract distribution. Just hammers, saws, sweat, and smiles. And at age 70, as he swings his hammer he and his friends feel they are being the Church.

Are they? Can a dozen guys rebuilding a widow's storm-shattered house be the Church? Of course they can. Indeed, they're being the Church outside the four walls of the church building, so they're being quite missional. But what if half of those guys are not born again? What if they're there just to feel better about themselves? Are they still being the Church?

The trap we fall into is that we're constantly looking to define the Church by what we do instead of by who is the Source of our doings. So we tend to look around and say, "The Church has been *this* way and we're not happy with the results. So let's swing the pendulum over *that* way. That will surely take us where we want to go."

And thus we have churches earnestly pursuing missional-ity as fast and hard as their earnest feet can carry them. And as others have been quick to point out, many are losing their grip on sound doctrine in the stampede, and thereby setting up the next reactionary pendulum swing.

In a sense, the Charismatic Renewal movement of the Seventies and Eighties set up the countervailing Neo-Reformed resurgence of the Nineties and "Oughts." Forty years ago some people looked around and said, "We've drifted too far from what the Church was in the First Century. We're not being the Church." So they concluded the remedy for that was returning to the gifts and miracles of the book of Acts. The result was a movement that ended up producing "megachurches" all over the world.

Then twenty years ago others made precisely the same observation: "We've drifted too far from the model of the First Century church. All these megachurches can't possibly be the ideal manifestation of the Church." And the "house church" movement was born.

The fact is, in every time and in every place, we find people pointing to the status quo and saying, "We're doing church wrong. We're being the Church wrong."

What we miss in this endless cycle of reform and counter-reform is the truth Jesus laid out in His parable. Amid the wheat, tares invariably grow. And a key source of our frustration is that we can never seem to put our fingers on that one, defining THING that, if we'll just all do that THING, then we'll be the Church just as the manufacturer intended.

This Holy Grail of Church-dom is elusive because we're seeking it in the wrong realm. We quest and search and tilt at windmills in the realm of first-order change, when the thing we're looking for is lying out in the open in the second-order realm. We search and search under the spreading branches of the Tree of the Knowledge of Good and Evil. And what we seek cannot, will not, ever be there.

No external standard, practice, emphasis or belief can ever make us the Church. The only thing that truly defines us as the Church is a connection to the Father of All Creation as Source. Is our life coming from Him, to us and through us? Are we a corporate entity comprised wholly and fully of People of the Way—not confined to a single building but scattered across the globe yet connected by a common Source of life and power?

The role and purpose of the Church is to be the conduit for bringing God's presence and transformative rule back into the planet. What is frustrating about this amazing truth is that it is so hard to articulate. Words literally fail. Any attempt at definition ends up narrowing it down to become something less than what it really is.

Which then leads me to what I love about it. The reality of what it means to be a part of this thing called the Church is better than anything we could possibly come up with on our own. It's not limited by organization. It's not limited by what we can know. It's not limited by the ways that we can structure, organize, and define it. It's only limited by the infinite One. And therefore it's unlimited.

> **"THE ROLE AND PURPOSE OF THE CHURCH IS TO BE THE CONDUIT FOR BRINGING GOD'S PRESENCE AND TRANSFORMATIVE RULE BACK INTO THE PLANET."**

Let me say it again: God's mission is to cover all of creation with His glorious nature. But the wonder is that His chosen instruments for carrying out that mission are you and me. It is the Church that will display God to a waiting, watching, aching world. As we receive, contain and broadcast God's glory in this natural world, it will even be a revelation in the realms of angels. Paul hints at this in Ephesians 3 in a passage about the freshly revealed "mystery of Christ" (v. 4). He continues …

> To me, the very least of all saints, this grace was given, to preach to the Gentiles the unfathomable riches of Christ, and to bring to light what is the **administration of the mystery** which for ages has been hidden in God who created all things; **so that the manifold wisdom of God might now be made known through the church to the rulers and the authorities in the Heavenly places.** This was in accordance with the eternal purpose which He carried out in Christ Jesus our Lord, in whom we have boldness and **confident access** through faith in Him. (v. 8-12)

The long hidden mystery to which Paul refers, concealed in the types and shadows of Old Testament feasts and Levitical regulations, was that God would use a corporate body of humans ("the church"), operating with Him as their Source ("confident access"), to display and spread His restoring, healing, curse-repealing glory ("the manifold wisdom of God") throughout *both* of the realms born-again believers inhabit—the visible and invisible.

Yes, we who contain and broadcast His nature are the Church. Sometimes the Church, in a corporate sense, will retreat for a season to come aside and receive from Him. And sometimes the Church, reinvigorated and full of fresh purpose, will advance and begin to take more territory. And neither the retreat or the advance makes them the Church. What makes them the Church is their source.

Here, however, is where things get sticky. How do we lead such a collection of God-connected, God-sourced individuals? After all, there is only one Head of the Church. But isn't there a legitimate need to organize the church in some way? I certainly think so.

We're about to turn a corner in our journey.

A PARABLE—
PART VI

The Game went on everywhere. Fields and parks, anywhere there was a bit of green grass, people figured out how to play and draw others into the joy and excitement of playing. No one really seemed to be in charge of organizing this; it just grew.

The other two groups continued to figure out how to maintain their existence and influence. Organizations grew. With each generation and every cultural shift, leaders proposed new ideas.

New songs in one group—even a whole new style of songs. Creative teaching in the other group, building momentum and expectation with every known strategy they could lay their hands on.

Sometimes interested Players would attend the teaching or attend the events and deeply enjoy the encouragement and the intriguing thoughts. They would sit in chairs right alongside people who thought they were actually playing The Game. As if the lesson, the song, the cheers were The Game itself.

If you had never played, you had no way to know.

These groups came in all shapes and sizes, and some drew crowds and some did not. Players would leave these meetings and go to the edge of town to enjoy The Game. Non-players would return home after the meetings and wonder why such a life-changing Game was not changing their life.

It was a strange co-existence between those who played The Game and those who believed they were playing as they attended these encouraging meetings.

CHAPTER 7

TARGETS OF A SPIRITUAL LEADER

"If I find in myself desires which nothing in this world can satisfy the only logical explanation is that I was made for another world."
—C. S. Lewis

"No doubt we will always feel the tug between the two worlds, for human beings comprise an odd combination of the two. We find ourselves stuck in the middle: angels wallowing in mud, mammals attempting to fly."
—Philip Yancey, Rumors of Another World

A season of change—maybe even of reformation—is upon us as Christian leaders. Shifts in every imaginable world system are in progress all around the planet. I am convinced that we, the Church, have an unprecedented opportunity to lead this change. As we begin to look specifically at the targets of a spiritual leader, I want to begin this section by laying out three perspectives that I believe can help provide a crucial plumb line as we navigate this season. These perspectives are woven all through the fabric of this book, but it is now time to state them explicitly.

The first perspective is one of the most recurrent themes of this book. That is, we live not only in a material realm, but also in a spiritual realm. These two realms are related, connected, and even integrated. The interplay between these two realms constitutes the territory in which a spiritual leader operates. The connection between these two realms must be familiar to any man or woman who would attempt to lead people in the ways of God's Kingdom.

This reality is the backdrop to all other realities, and without a clear and consistent understanding of this stage, we may easily and understandably lead well in one realm to the exclusion or even harm of the operation of the other.

The second theme is that God declares the end from the beginning. A familiar passage in Isaiah establishes this paradigm. God Himself says:

> *"Remember the former things long past, For I am God, and there is no other; I am God, and there is no one like Me, Declaring the end from the beginning, And from ancient times things which have not been done, Saying, 'My purpose will be established, And I will accomplish all My good pleasure.'"* (Isaiah 46:9-10)

Embedded here is a blueprint for us as we consider leading in the things and the ways of this God who declares the end from the beginning. For years I took comfort in these words, assured that God was in control, and that He knew the end, before the story ever started. But in recent days, I have begun to see that in this passage there is more than just the comfort afforded us in God's Sovereign perspective. He is handing us a way to understand what He is up to.

First, I realized that the idea was one of declaration, not simply knowledge. God is not simply telling me He knows what is coming; He is telling me that He is still creating by speaking. He is declaring the end. Just as planets once emanated from His uttered word, He is still creating the yet-to-come end. The end, the wrap up of this whole story, is still flowing from His lips. It is coming, as sure as the worlds that were once created.

Most importantly though is when I began to realize that the preposition "from" has more than one meaning. The word "from" can mean "at this point," or, at the beginning, God declares what is coming. But the word "from" can also refer to Source; that from which something is derived.

We can legitimately, and I think necessarily, read this in this way. God is speaking into existence the end of the story, and His source for the end of time is the way it was in the beginning. God is restoring that which once was. God is not simply creating something that has never existed; He is bringing a new thing, fashioned after the first thing. God is restoring to the creation

His original design. Heaven and Earth were once one place; it will be again. Man lived in perfect unity with His God; He will again. Adam and Eve were in perfect unity, and were the stewards of all creation. We will be again.

The New Heavens and the New Earth are the renewed Heavens and the renewed Earth, returned to their factory settings. God is declaring the end, from the blueprint of the beginning. This crucial perspective helps us to partner more effectively with God's plan, because we can look back and see what once was as a model for what is coming.

The third perspective can been seen when Matthew tells us a fantastic story in Chapter 22 of his gospel. Jesus is confronted by the Sadducees who, in one more attempt to trap the Author of reality, ask Jesus a question. The set up for this question begins like this: a man married a woman, and then he died. His brother married her, and he died; his brother married her and he died, and so on. (I've always wanted to call this the parable of the unwise siblings. And don't you know there is a grieving mother somewhere shouting at the remaining brothers. "No, don't do it...?")

Anyway, after seven brothers meet their fate in holy matrimony to this woman, the Sadducees ask Jesus this question. "With whom will this woman be united in the resurrection?" Jesus' answer is classic. He says, "You are mistaken, not understanding the Scriptures nor the power of God." He answers and tells experts in scripture that they do not understand scripture, and His supporting argument is that these men do not understand the power of God. Translation: they think of the scriptures from the perspective of Earth, rather than the perspective of Heaven. In the classic mistake of a child who thinks life began when he was born, the Sadducees apply their thought processes to scripture with an Earth-centric perspective.

Jesus' rebuke points us to this third and crucial perspective. We must learn to think from the Heavens down, and not simply from the Earth up. From the Earth up, we think of God coming to rescue us from this planet. From the Heavens down, we realize that He is unfolding a larger plan, and we just get to play.

From the Earth up, we think about what we must do to please God. From the Heavens down we recognize what He has done to prepare us. From the Earth up we see too small a picture and run the risk of thinking that this is a story about us. From the Heavens down, the story of a great Father and Redeemer includes His children and the redeemed, but is a far bigger story than simply rescuing humans from discomfort and damnation.

Looking through the lenses of these three crucial perspectives help us shift from simply leading an organization to realizing that we are leading a

Kingdom and a movement. With these three perspectives, our motives and our actions shift to think more like a spiritual parent than a child of the Earth.

SHIFT THE RIGHT THING

One way to think about the targets of a spiritual leader is to say that we are moving people from one place or one way of thinking to another place or way of thinking. Helping people to shift in these ways ought to be not only a priority for a spiritual leader, but without these shifts we may actually urge our followers to move in ways and directions that are significantly different from the ways and purposes of God's Kingdom. The following shifts are central to the movement of a spiritual leader.

1. **SHIFT FROM A NATURAL WORLDVIEW TO AN INTEGRATED WORLDVIEW**

   This is one of the keys to this entire book; perhaps more importantly, this is one of the key distinctives to Jesus' teaching and ministry. Jesus tells Nicodemus in John 3 that while most people have only been Earthbound, Jesus has been in both Heaven and Earth. His point is that people struggle to believe Him about the issues of Earth and will not be able to make the shift to believe the Heavenly things He teaches.

   As long as our senses are our only way of taking in reality, as long as we only have a material view of reality, we will always be quickly deceived and wrongly focused. Not simply the Gospels, but the entire Bible is based on a worldview where both the material realm and the spiritual realm exist. Not only do they exist, but they are also inter-related in ways that form the territory of spiritual leadership and the thesis of this book.

   We must always be moving people to first acknowledge and recognize, but secondly to grow in familiarity with, the spiritual realm. It is this single issue that makes us as spiritual leaders different from any other type of leader. It is this shift that defines a leader as a spiritual leader.

2. **SHIFT FROM DOING *FOR* GOD, TO DOING *FROM* GOD**

   Once people make the shift from a natural worldview to an integrated worldview, it is a natural, yet crucial shift to help people recognize that God is the initiator and we are the receiver, not the other way around.

Jesus gives the crowd a paradigm shifting truth when He says, *"The son of Man did not come to be served, but to serve, and to give His life as a ransom for many"* (Matthew 20:28). It is a clear statement that we need what God is doing; He does not need what we are doing.

Luke says in Acts 17 that the God who created us does not need anything from us, as He is not served by human hands.

So much freedom can be found in this one simple shift. God is acting on our behalf. He is not calling us to accomplish tasks for Him. Any task He is invested in could be completed with a breath. God is invested in moving through people, not getting people to move on *His behalf.*

So often we think that God wants to receive while we initiate. That is a direct fruit of the Knowledge of Good and Evil at work. He is the Author, the Alpha, and the Finisher, the Omega. When we realize we exist to receive all that God is and all He gives, it frees us to stop trying to do that which is impossible for us to do.

This simple yet profound shift makes Grace and Power available to men and women, because it helps people to rely rightly on God's power and provision instead of their own.

Listen to the language of a leader. You will quickly learn if he is expecting people to perform for God, or if he understands that people are made to receive from God. One puts the burden on people, the other puts the burden squarely on God. This shift will move people to use words like "surrender" and "receive" instead of words like "strive" and "work."

3. SHIFT FROM LEARNING AND APPLYING PRINCIPLES TO HEARING AND SURRENDERING TO THE VOICE OF GOD

When people try to work "for" God, all of the emphasis is on what people can do in their own strength on behalf of an omnipotent God. The emphasis is subtly (or not so subtly) placed on man's willpower and capacity to get "right principles." In this mindset, education, motivation and inspiration become the key strategies for creating disciples.

As people make the shift to operating "from" God, the emphasis shifts from emphasizing Man's capabilities to emphasizing God's ability, availability, and willingness to operate. God speaks, men receive and follow. God initiates, men cooperate and receive His Presence and His work.

> "AGAIN, THIS IS A VERY IMPORTANT SHIFT FOR A SPIRITUAL LEADER TO MAKE, AS THE EMPHASIS ON EDUCATION AND MOTIVATION IS ACTUALLY HUMANISM."

Again this is a very important shift for a spiritual leader to make, as the emphasis on education and motivation is actually humanism. Rather than truly demonstrate what God can and desires to do, this emphasis demonstrates the cleverness and sufficiency of the human race.

God's voice actually contains the resource and power to complete that which it describes. The same voice that said "planets" resulted in planets. When we expect God to give instructions and have people follow with their intelligence and willpower only, we end up with ideas about planets, but no real celestial activity.

4. SHIFT FROM AN EMPHASIS ON OUTWARD BEHAVIOR TO AN EMPHASIS ON IDENTITY AND BELIEFS

We see throughout the book of Proverbs and multiple other Scripture addresses that God looks on the inside, at the motive, while man looks on the outside. Whether addressing an individual or a culture, we must direct people to not simply focus on what they do, but rather to understand who they are.

The heart, the wellspring of all life, is the target of all transformation and all Spirit-inspired motivation. When we focus on the outside without understanding the inside, we create law, and ultimately failure and shame.

When we lead people to understand their inner life and how to connect to the proper Source, we move them toward relationship and ultimately freedom.

As a man tryeth in his heart so is he? As a man laboreth in his heart so is he? No, scripture is clear. *"As a man believes in his heart"* (Proverbs 23:7). We move people toward substantial change when we lead them to focus on belief and identity instead of outward behavior and performance.

Early on, we discussed the importance of being sure that leadership is taught with appropriate context; specifically, that if a spiritual leader does not know the targets and territory of leading, they may actually work contrary to their intent. With this in mind, let's summarize key truths we have uncovered regarding the targets and territory of a spiritual leader.

BI-LOCATIONAL LEADERS

In ministry we use the term "bi-vocational" to refer to people who make their income one way so that they can do "ministry" without depending on it for income. One of our main thrusts in this book is to make clear this one simple yet extremely significant issue: spiritual leaders lead people who inhabit two realms simultaneously. You could say we are "bi-locational."

As mentioned above, the material realm and the spiritual realm are intertwined, and this integration provides the context for a completed worldview and definition of reality. The most basic issue for a spiritual leader is to be aware of, and know how to operate in the spiritual realm.

Helping people to understand and operate within this "two-realm" context is the primary territory for a spiritual leader. Without this backdrop, all of our best leading and teaching simply becomes superstition and law. Teaching people how to live spiritual lives with only the material world in mind sets us up for ongoing and growing misunderstandings and misapplications of the practices of our faith. Like simply trying to envision a new configuration of deck chairs without realizing that the larger world of the Titanic is moving toward a certain destiny, when we teach people about spiritual things from a purely material worldview, all we teach them is how to manipulate the material world.

Teaching people to operate in an integrated world also helps people to differentiate between which things are eternal and which things are temporary. It teaches people to see and think more like God, with eternal goals in mind. It teaches people to see people in their proper context, as spiritual beings, in the Image of God, on a human journey to return to their eternal existence. Teaching people to think from an integrated perspective brings the freedom of being able to access an invisible power source that can change everything in the visible world.

This crucial map of reality, two co-existent realms with two sets of integrated operating systems, must be the backdrop for any leader who would desire to lead Kingdom endeavors.

LEADING PEOPLE TO ENCOUNTER GOD

If the primary territory is an integrated worldview, then the primary target of a spiritual leader is to lead people into an encounter with the God who created all things. "Seek first the Kingdom" must become "seek first the King." If we lead people to anything less, we pass on a deceptive legacy that says God is not with us.

While any number of important tasks, endeavors, initiatives and so on may fit into our strategy, if at the core of what we do we do not lead people to encounter God for themselves, we not only fail them, but we teach them to set their sights wrongly. Keep in mind I am not referring to leading such an encounter in our services or events only. I am talking about leading our coworkers, our subordinates, our children into encountering God in a daily sort of way. Leading people around us into the recognition that encountering God is not a big event sort of thing, but a way of life.

I had a friend who told me once of a church plant. Two families left all they knew and moved to a community, believing they were called to begin a church there. This is not so hard to believe. What was difficult for me to comprehend was the scene my friend described. Two married couples and their children (young teenagers) sat in pews while one of the fathers stood behind a large pulpit and preached. To five people. Three of whom shared his last name.

It was almost as if they had relegated encountering God to a religious form that looked like a church service. The people must sit quietly while the guy in charge must preach a message.

What if, in day-to-day conversation we learn, and more importantly demonstrate, that God is the other Person in the conversation? When Jesus turned His eyes upward and spoke to the Father, He showed that God was as much a part of that exchange as the humans gathered around.

What if the way we strategize involved asking God for His ideas? What if the way we handle conflict involved letting God speak? What if His voice was invited to our staff meetings? Our re-cap meetings? Not just a perfunctory prayer to begin, but actually asking His input. And then waiting for it.

If we do not recognize on the front end that we exist to help others encounter God, we will chase after principles and values, all to the exclusion of the Source of all things. If we do not lead our own people to encounter God as a part of their day-to-day function, how can we expect meaningful encounter to be the outcome?

The most important thing you can do as a spiritual leader is to lead people into an encounter. Not new ideas. Not more passion. Not a fresh vision. An encounter. With God.

LEADING PEOPLE INTO IDENTITY

In a genuine encounter with the Source of all Being, every human has an opportunity to deeply discover their truest self and their deepest purpose. Though it is not "about us," the story of the Greatest Father Ever must by necessity also be about His children. We exist to receive and contain Him. We exist to broadcast Him. This can only happen through encounter. It certainly cannot happen through education alone.

In connection to God, people become their best and truest selves. It is amazing what you can get out of someone who is loosed to become themselves. Far more than motivation and vision casting, a person who is loosed to become themselves will change their environment and ultimately their culture.

The importance of matching a person with their calling is crucial. If you discover someone who was made to worship and turn them loose to do so, they and everyone around them will flourish. If you find someone who was made to administrate, their tasks will drip with aliveness.

> "TEACHING PEOPLE TO THINK FROM AN INTEGRATED PERSPECTIVE BRINGS THE FREEDOM OF BEING ABLE TO ACCESS AN INVISIBLE POWER SOURCE THAT CAN CHANGE EVERYTHING IN THE VISIBLE WORLD."

Conversely, if you find someone who was made to nurture people and task them with stacking boxes, they will wither. You might even consider them to be a poor employee. More than a proper seat on a bus, our willingness to discover what God has deposited in our people and help to turn it loose will give our productivity Power.

The idea that we are to "train up a child in the way he should go" (Proverbs 22:6) really means to discover in what way your child was made to go, and help him fulfill it. It is a human and material worldview that says that "the way he should go" is determined by our ideas as parents. This concept has much more to do with discovering and unleashing Original Design than it does getting people to conform to external standards. Help a child discover who he is and when he is old he will not depart from it.

Help a follower discover who they are and they will follow you, because you are showing them what is possible for them. There is no salary or benefit package that can motivate people more than discovering their true self.

FREEDOM AND TRANSFORMATION

From encounter to identity is a path. And that path is the journey of freedom and transformation that the gospel invitation is all about. If we are to lead people to become themselves it also involves helping them discover who they are not. A significant part of the journey towards freedom includes overcoming lies and false self-image.

If we only lead people to perform and act, we may actually inadvertently support the very false self-image that stands in the way of their true identity. It is so crucial to really know the people we lead. If we know nothing about their personal life, we are walking in a minefield.

All of us are on a journey of overcoming and becoming. All of us have triggers and histories that set us up for certain propensities. Strengths AND weaknesses. Just as we must know our own triggers and learn our own soul, we must also begin to learn the journey of the people we lead.

If I, as a male leader, have no idea how my employees experienced family, I really don't know yet how they perceive me, or how they receive my leadership. If I do not know something about their journey or life, I may experience insubordination when the issue is really fear. Or I may experience laziness when the issue is really a father wound. If we do not have the skills or discernment to recognize these things we must find a way to realize that all of our people—ourselves included—are on a journey to become who we really are. If this is the case, we are also on a journey to overcome the lies we have believed, the wounds we have received, and the voices that plague us.

People who followed Jesus found release from such things. What if the people who followed us actually received lies and criticism from us, instead of relief from a world where such pain is inflicted? We might actually empower the complete opposite kingdom of the one we were hoping for.

We must learn to help our people walk a path of freedom. Jesus, as a leader, set captives free. Let's be sure that we do not lead people back in to captivity. In fact, let us also, like the One we follow, lead people out of the chains that hold them.

SEEING OLD THINGS IN NEW WAYS

"Repent," Jesus said, and the objective was that His followers would see and experience the Kingdom that was in their midst. The problem, or at least the problem that kept them from seeing the problem, was that they looked with old eyes at a new thing. Clearly, as was discussed in the chapter on The Problem Jesus Came to Solve, those who followed Jesus had to change their whole perceptual framework to really grasp His message. More so, they had to make this shift to truly receive the Kingdom.

Repentance means to change the way we take in reality. Like looking through a new prescription for our glasses, everything we have previously seen now looks different. The change in us allows us to see the world and the Kingdom around us in new ways.

It is important that the God who never changes and His Gospel never get old. More so, it is important that the Person and the Message never get so familiar that we lose that gratitude and awe that comes from the Presence of Life-Changing Truth. One of the greatest compliments to me as a teacher is when veterans of the church world come to me after a teaching and say, "I have never heard that before." But the truth is that there is no new truth.

We must be able to look from new angles, use new words, see new perspectives without relinquishing the solid anchor of unchanging Truth.

We must help people repent. We must lead people to see old things in new ways. If the disciples could not see new things because of old eyes, then what if we could help people see through new eyes? Everything would seem, and would function as if, new.

A spiritual leader must recognize that the One who never changes is also new every morning. That the Ancient of Days also came as an infant. A spiritual leader must know that if God is truly Infinite, then flowing from His Being is newness every second. Helping people to see in a world that is material and deteriorating requires opening the eyes of our hearts to a world which is soaked in revelation and is being made new.

Seeing that, we must then lead others to see.

CHANGING THE ATMOSPHERE

An organizational leader can hire and fire, a spiritual leader can speak to storms and demons. When we begin to realize that spiritual leadership is the restoration of God's original assignment to take dominion over the creation, we can think differently about our assignment. Our assignment was not to set up governmental or organizational structures, it was to establish the Presence and Nature of God in the geography we inhabit.

Whether the storm we speak to is a literal weather phenomenon or a room full of confusion and chaos, we must see that we have the ability to change the atmosphere. If you have ever walked into a room where someone is angry, have you noticed that their anger fills the room in an almost tangible way? You can feel it, much like you can feel the physical temperature. We all have the ability to "take dominion," or to transmit what is in us. Whether we use that power for good or for harm is up to us.

In Matthew 10, Jesus is giving instructions to his disciples about taking what He has given them to the surrounding community. As He describes how to interact with households He tells them, *"And if the house is worthy, let your peace come upon it, but if it is not worthy, let your peace return to you"* (v. 13).

It seems He is telling them that they have some say so about whether or not they allow that which is within them to fill the atmosphere around them, or to remain within them. It seems that He is telling them that the atmosphere around them is something that they can affect.

Imagine someone who, in the midst of confusion or conflict can simply "let their peace come upon it." Or someone who in a time of rapid change can "let their peace come upon it." More than just peace, we all know people we look forward to interacting with because of what we seem to receive simply by being in their presence. Those people understand whether consciously or unconsciously that "freely they have received, freely they can give."

A spiritual leader may or may not occupy a position of authority in any given setting, but he or she recognizes that they can lead the atmosphere in a room. They realize that they can lead the hearts of people to contain more of the things that are true about God. It is fascinating to watch a spiritual leader who does *not* occupy the position of authority in a given setting, but to see him or her still impacting the atmosphere. Sometimes it is the smallest thing, but they still leave their mark.

Love, joy, peace, patience, kindness, goodness, gentleness, meekness, mercy, and self-control are the fruits of the Spirit listed in Galatians 5, and these are the elements that occupy the atmosphere around a spiritual leader who has learned how to take dominion over the atmosphere. The question is not whether or not they can run a meeting; the question is whether or not more of God was breathed into the meeting itself and those who attended.

PEOPLE FOLLOW YOU

When you display the skills and characteristics described above, people follow you. They do not follow you simply because you occupy a position or carry a title. They follow because they trust. They follow because they receive life and fullness when they do.

You will see in the next chapter that certain types of organizations are lead by people with this type of interpersonal influence. Rather than lead from a place of position or title, you will see as an example how the Apache Indians were lead more by loosely affiliated spiritual leaders than by a singular "chief." People followed them because they were trusted. Such men were spread throughout the tribes, and if the enemies killed one of them, many times, several more rose up in their place.

Spiritual leaders gain followers because people around them see what is being described in this section. People around them encounter God. People around them become more their true self. People around them are seen and valued, and are drawn down a path of freedom and transformation. With or without title, these experiences will draw people.

It is for this reason that a developing spiritual leader must be careful to rightly relate to authorities and organizations around him. Like Absalom, it is possible to steal the hearts of people when they do not belong to you. When you do, you become divisive. Like Saul, it is possible to begin to use this influence from a place of insecurity. When you do, you become destructive. Like Herod, it is possible to use this influence selfishly. When you do, you become controlling. Never is it more clear that we give away what is inside us than when people see us and begin to follow.

People follow a spiritual leader with or without position or title. Often, how a budding leader uses this influence will actually determine whether or not position or title will follow. In an ideal setting, spiritual leaders also become positional leaders. It is still both true and valuable, however, that a growing organization will have spiritual leaders at all levels of hierarchy. Sometimes the lowest man on the totem pole can have great spiritual authority.

ONLY A SPIRITUAL LEADER

While leadership in both kingdoms is essential in a growing organization, and great managers are necessary, spiritual leaders will have a thumb on the pulse of some things that a material or organizational leader may not even acknowledge, or see. It is the necessity of the skill or sensitivity of spiritual leadership that really anchors the church or a believing group, business or family to the things that are central to our faith.

THE PRESENCE

We have said that the center of the target for us, the number one thing, is leading people to encounter God. Engaging, fostering, facilitating—whatever word we want to use here—connecting people to the presence of God requires awareness and sensitivity to God and His movements in any given moment. In a purely material mindset, people might talk about emotion or atmosphere, but a spiritual leader recognizes and responds to this simple yet central reality: God is with us.

Without this awareness, we can talk *about* God. We can talk about principles. We can educate, motivate, or inspire, but we cannot help people to connect. Like the parable, for those who have never played The Game, it is impossible to engage people around you in an experience that you cannot discern.

This intangible but palpable thing, or experience that we call (and rightly so) the Presence of God, is *the* thing that makes us the Church. Not our collective doctrines. Not our practices, or creeds. God being with us is the central thing that defines us as the Church.

If a leader cannot learn to facilitate, recognize and engage God in His Presence he will simply become an overseer. Not only is it important to take the stance that if God does not go, we will not go without Him, but we must learn that when He *does* go, it is imperative to move with Him.

One day, I taught a class on Hearing God Speak, with about a hundred people in the room. When teaching on this, I always talk about the nature of the Word of God and how it is so much more than simply right information or accurate direction. The Word of God is Creative and Living and Active and Powerful.

I began to talk about Colossians 1 and how in Christ (who is the Word), all things hold together. I began to see a connection in that moment, so I just spoke out loud what I saw. I said, "If in Him all things hold together, then the further we are from the Word, the more things begin to fall apart."

As I spoke this phrase, something happened in the room. I mean, nothing happened—but something happened. It was as if the atmosphere shifted. Like the thermostat kicked on, but it was not a temperature shift. As the shift grew, I saw faces begin to shift. In some cases, tears started to fall. The tugging inside me increased.

I looked down at my notes that I had not finished. And most of me wanted to get right back to my notes. I am a teacher, and I had an assignment: teach about Hearing God. Inwardly I began to consider my next point and felt like I had a rope tied to my guts. I could go on, but it felt … not right. What *was* right was unclear.

I wrestled a bit, because the most concrete thing to do (and the most comfortable thing to do) would be to resume my class. But it became clear, as more than just a stirring, that God was not intent on me finishing my class. He was doing something, and He had not warned me or asked my permission. Not only that, He did not tell me *what* He was doing.

I at least knew enough to not continue, so I just tried to get still and practice the very thing I was teaching. I tried to hear or discern or see or understand what He was doing in that moment.

I opted to ask the room, as I knew I was in a room full of others who also hear God. After hearing several people speak up, my wife, who was in the back of the room, raised her hand. She said she had a picture in her mind of people's hips. I don't know how else to describe this, but this feedback seemed to have the most weight, the most juice, the most connection to the moment that I had heard before.

I asked if anyone in the room had a need for healing in their hips and about a dozen hands went up. I had each of them stand, and we began to pray, agreeing with whatever God seemed to already be doing. Before we were done, several women had immediately noticeable healing in their hips. Pain was banished and range of motion was restored. Over the weeks ahead, we heard more stories of just what had happened in that moment.

What I learned that day was this: I am not in charge. I am certain I could have continued with my notes and finished the class. But we would have missed out on an opportunity to experience the Presence of God in a meaningful and powerful way.

A spiritual leader must learn to recognize, to follow, to be moved by this intangible yet palpable personal God, who may show up unannounced, or may not show up when we most expect Him to. We must learn to prioritize something that we have no control over. We must learn to seek first something that we cannot define, or manipulate.

But the bottom line is that a leader who is materially minded will not even know to look for that which is most important and central to us, the Presence of God Himself.

DISCERNMENT

One of the most important characteristics a spiritual leader must develop is discernment. We see in 1 Corinthians 12 that one of the gifts Paul mentions is the discernment of spirits. A ground level interpretation of that could have us on a "search and identify" mission for types of demons; but I believe that the most important function of that gift, and a crucial function of a spiritual leader, is not just to identify evil spirits but to recognize and discern the Spirit of God.

Look at a tragic moment in Israel's history. In Ezekiel chapter 10, the priests show up for work one day, but God Himself decides He will not be attending church that day. This seems kind of important.

That day, the only thing that changes in the functioning of the temple is that God departs. The people and the priests go about their regular routines, and for various reasons, take no note of the departure of God Himself.

What a tragedy it would be if we have so learned our craft, so practiced our routines, and so honed our strategies, that we can do them with—or without—God.

In this moment in Israel's history, the most important thing about the temple was not the activities of the priests, but the Presence of God. If we are excellent at our tasks, but lack the discernment to recognize God in His exquisite movements, we can miss the target entirely.

Central to this thing called spiritual leadership is awareness of this thing called "spirit." And central to this realm called "spiritual" is the Spirit of God Himself. What He is doing (or not doing) in any given moment must be the guiding factor in all the movement and activity of a spiritual leader.

Without discernment, we are all driving blind. And while I hear that the blind *can* lead the blind, I recommend against it.

PRAYER AND FASTING

With this difficult to define first priority, we discover that we must prioritize activities that seem to look like doing nothing. Times spent in silence and physical inactivity become the most important activities of one who would propose to lead in this invisible endeavor. Times in which we become sensitized to interacting with the invisible. Times in which we learn the ways of the Invisible One. Times in which we learn our role in this invisible place called the Kingdom of God, and discover how the invisible activities have dominion over the visible ones.

Prayer. Interacting with, communicating with, receiving from, complaining to, communicating wonder to an invisible, sonically silent God.

If we are to lead in both Kingdoms, we must learn how to be inhabitants of both Kingdoms. We must learn how to interact with the invisible the same way a new driver has to learn how to drive in snow or rain. It is a different environment with different governing realities.

We are more familiar with our minds than with our spirit. We are more in tune with our will than with His Spirit. We are more comfortable with reason than with faith. Prayer is that activity where these things change.

Similarly, the activity of fasting is a place where these crucial shifts can also occur. When we approach fasting with a material view we too easily see it as we do many other spiritual disciplines. With a material mindset, fasting can seem to be a bargaining chip, a statement of commitment, or a method of buying influence with God.

While it is clear that fasting has an impact in the spiritual realm, a significant part of that has to do with helping us to make those shifts. Shifting our own familiarity and focus from the material realm, and the material *us*, to the spiritual realm, and the spiritual us.

For a material or organizational leader, again, such activities (or non-activities) will appear to have no value, or only soul-ish value. What appears to be cessation of activity to a material leader is actually commencing spiritual activity to one who has eyes to see and ears to hear. In fact these non-activities are where we develop those eyes and ears.

One of my most consistent prayers is Paul's prayer in Ephesians 1: *Lord, open the eyes of our heart, and give us the spirit of wisdom and revelation.* Our need to operate in the invisible realm is high, and it depends to a great degree on which set of senses we operate from.

Prayer and fasting develop in us our familiarity with operating in an invisible world.

SPIRITUAL WARFARE

Now that we begin to cease from material activity and enter into spiritual activity, we begin to get a glimpse of something that Paul writes of often. We are on a battleground at all times, and the battle is not one of flesh and blood. We wrestle against *"the rulers, against the powers, against the world forces of this darkness, against the spiritual forces of wickedness in the Heavenly places"* (Ephesians 6:12).

Another area that a materially minded leader will not even see and certainly will not engage is the reality that we are in a spiritual war.

When we approach this idea with a material worldview, we will tend to fall prey to one of two specific mindsets. We will either become superstitious, or complacent. While we can agree that what Paul wrote is true, thinking about spiritual warfare from a material mindset I believe has often paralyzed the church.

Superstition is the mindset that looks for formulas that force the spiritual world to respond to us a certain way. Repeating phrases, our tone or the volume of our voice—all these and more are the things of magic and superstition. The spiritual realm is not a set of forces for us to manipulate. It is a reality that we must learn to navigate. We must learn that our thoughts and the condition of our hearts have an affect on and empower things in the spiritual realm. More so than any activity, the content and condition of our heart empowers one kingdom or another.

Complacency is the opposite trap. When we approach the spiritual war from a material view, we can intellectualize our experience and use intelligence, knowledge and reason to fight a battle that is spiritual in nature. When we simply rest in our own knowledge, we actually become complacent about the war itself.

I have often thought about the difference between the United States and Israel in the way that we think about war. If you travel the Holy Land, you will see that any member of the Israeli Defense Forces carries their weapon with them at all times. This open and ongoing display of military readiness is simply a way of life. The likelihood that a skirmish can break out anytime, anywhere, in a city or highway or a bus for that matter is an ongoing threat. The Israelis do not operate in fear, simply in readiness.

Conversely, it's easy to grow complacent in the us. One of the reasons that the 9/11 attacks were so shocking to us is the sense of safety we had falsely cultivated. Our soil is off limits to enemies, or so we once believed.

We can grow complacent when our view of the material world is filled with what appear to be "riches," as they are here in the us. When this is our landscape, we too easily overlook the poverty of the spiritual realm around us. What does it profit a man if he is rich in the visible, but loses sight of all things invisible?

The preparedness of the spiritual leader, to always be on guard without becoming fearful or superstitious, is a crucial part of engaging the war.

Leaders often shy away from the teaching and practices of spiritual warfare because of things they have seen others do, or even mindsets they have seen in other groups. What you see is a classic schism where the superstitious prove the point of the complacent, and the complacent prove the point of the superstitious. Each justifies their stance because of the other. We change the wrong thing, and end up without a healthy view of remaining engaged in something that Paul seemed to constantly remind us about.

I believe balance and authority will come from restoring not just awareness of the war, but a worldview that makes the war neither weird nor intellectual. Understanding the connection between the spiritual and the natural world and practicing the integration of the two realms and our role in those realms gives us a way to think about spiritual warfare that is healthy and available to us all.

The issue at hand is still to determine who or what is the *source* for the human soul. When Adam and Eve changed our source to the Knowledge of Good and Evil, our primary (only) source of reality became our senses. When our senses became our source of reality, knowledge and reason became our process, or our way. This practically put the god of this world in charge of how we learn and how we see. We live by evidence and reason, and Satan is in charge of evidence. With self as source, we will always tend toward empowering the wrong kingdom.

The key issue in spiritual warfare then, is to not let circumstances dictate to us which voice we will listen to. In the worst moments, and in the best moments, we must let God be our source and our way. We must use our will to choose His voice in every moment. We win the war when regardless of circumstance we allow God to be our source.

Simply put, the war is about choosing which voice we will listen to in any given moment. Which brings us to the last idea of things that a spiritual leader must lead in, because no one else will.

HEARING GOD SPEAK

Throughout these last sections, I have written about things that have a built-in assumption. Every section above assumes, presumes and presupposes that God is speaking and His people are receiving. This idea is given treatment throughout this book, in a variety of places. The reason for this is that this is the primary activity of any believer, therefore the primary area of leadership for a spiritual leader.

Much of my teaching is about ideas, paradigms, and new ways of thinking. As a result, I am often asked the question, "Yeah, but what should I DO?"

The answer to the question is this one single practice: hear God and teach others to do the same. It's the highest, most powerful and most vital target of a spiritual leader.

CHAPTER 8

THE REORGANIZED CHURCH OF THE EVERLASTING STARFISH

"If you build it, they will come."
—Field of Dreams

"And I, when I am lifted up from the Earth, will draw all people to myself."
—Jesus of Nazareth

We now know that the assassination of Abraham Lincoln was not the work of a lone zealot. History sleuths have uncovered a large cast of conspirators in which the actor John Wilkes Booth was merely playing the lead. The original grand plan of the conspiracy was to not only kill the President but also Vice-President Andrew Johnson and Secretary of State William Seward— disrupting the entire presidential line of succession and throwing the nation into chaos. The military strategist types have a term for this type of attack, had the full plan been successful. It goes by the grisly name "decapitation strike." It describes an attack designed to eliminate an enemy's command and control mechanisms. Today, smart governments (and smart organizations) take great pains to keep themselves from being vulnerable to a decapitation attack.

A few years ago I read a fascinating business management book called *The Starfish and the Spider: The Unstoppable Power of Leaderless Organizations* by Ori Brafman and Rod Beckstrom.

At the heart of the book's premise is an insight that has far-reaching implications for the way we approach organizing and leading the Church—local and universal.

The book describes two different models for organizational headship—the aforementioned starfish and spider. Spider organizations have a single head, with a body and legs that grow downward from, and are controlled by, the head. These are classic top-down, pyramidal, hierarchical organizations. Spider-structured organizations are highly vulnerable to decapitation attacks. If the head is cut off, the organization, deprived of leadership command, will quickly die. Examples of this include most modern businesses as well as numerous dictator-led governments, past and present.

In contrast, an actual starfish has legs but no discernible head. If you cut off any part of the starfish it will not die. In many cases, the part that is cut off will grow back. And often the detached piece can actually become a whole new starfish. In a similar way, starfish organizations have a decentralized leadership and a diffused command-and-control apparatus. This type of organization is rare but examples do exist. The Internet, by design, has a starfish structure. Certain nomadic people groups are led starfish style, as is the venerable and ubiquitous Alcoholics Anonymous movement.

In *The Starfish and the Spider*, these two types of organizations are compared and contrasted across a number of categories, including leadership style, distribution of knowledge, and even levels of control within the organization. The book goes on to make the case that starfish organizations cannot be stopped by the efforts of outsiders alone. In fact, for a number of reasons, this type of organization grows or even multiplies in the face of opposition.

Clearly the global Church (universal) is a starfish. This is why the church tends to flourish in times of persecution or pressure. Hostile conditions can actually spur growth in a starfish organization.

At the same time, most local expressions of the church are—by divine design—spiders. Spider organizations have a clear and specific leader upon whom the rest of the organization relies for direction and vision. They are led from the top down. Leaders in this type of organization sit at the top of a hierarchical order, and drive the organization from this position. As referenced earlier, the loss of this head usually results in diminishment or even death to the organization.

Leadership in a starfish organization flows from *influence* rather than hierarchical or positional authority. In their book, Brafman and Beckstrom point to the Apache Indians as an example of this model. Rather than being ruled by a single chief, the Apaches were led by the influence of numerous spiritual leaders. These men did not hold "positions" much as they simply had the trust and "ear" of the people. If one of these leaders were killed during an attack or invasion, one or more new leaders would simply arise in his place.

A very similar dynamic was in operation in the growth of the early church. Virtually all of Jesus' original disciples were martyred. The persecutors of the early church assumed that killing the leadership of the fledgling movement would kill the movement as well. The existence of nearly a billion Christians on planet Earth today suggests that they were mistaken. The decapitation strikes designed to put an end to the movement actually facilitated the spread of the church into the rest of the world as many new leaders emerged. Inspired by the devotion and the sacrifice of the saints, the ranks of those known as the People of the Way multiplied.

INVISIBLE LEADERSHIP

Here in the postmodern 21st Century, we must realize that Christianity is a belief system built upon a worldview that most people no longer hold and find utterly strange. The dominant worldview here in the Western hemisphere is a blinding blend of rationalism and materialism. I use these two terms in the philosophical sense. *Rationalism* refers to a belief that all truth can be obtained through human reason and intellect. If something can be known, the human mind can deduce it. *Materialism* is not about Madonna's "material girl"—seeking after riches and possessions. In philosophy, materialism refers to a belief that the material, natural world is all there is. This worldview is encapsulated in the late Carl Sagan's famous quote: "The Cosmos is all that is or was or ever will be."

These twin pillars of the modern approach to viewing life and the universe insist that we define reality by what we can know with our mind and interact with through our senses. Obviously, this worldview limits us to operating in the natural, visible realm only—because the natural, visible stuff is all there is and there ain't no more!

I referred to this as a "blinding blend" of philosophies because holding that worldview actually makes it almost impossible to see or perceive a broader, wider reality. In other words, if you really believe the natural, material world is all there is, you'll ignore, miss or dismiss any and all evidence of a separate, supernatural, invisible reality. It's a self-confirming deception.

In sharp contrast, the Bible, from beginning to end, makes a clear assumption that an invisible spiritual realm exists, and is just as real as the visible one. In fact, the invisible realm is portrayed as being the one that preceded the visible and is higher than it—has authority over it. Furthermore, the invisible realm is eternal whereas the material world is, to use the King James Bible word, temporal—which means it is malleable, changeable and elements of it will eventually pass away. In other words, the invisible realm is actually *more real* than the one we perceive with our natural senses. It's only our nature-based perception that makes it seem less so.

> **"IN OTHER WORDS, THE INVISIBLE REALM IS ACTUALLY MORE REAL THAN THE ONE WE PERCEIVE WITH OUR NATURAL SENSES. IT'S ONLY OUR NATURE-BASED PERCEPTION THAT MAKES IT SEEM LESS SO."**

As believers, we've long known and taught that we hold "dual citizenship." We've understood that we are citizens of a natural nation here on Earth and—once we're reborn of God (reconnected to the originally intended Source)—we are citizens of a Heavenly kingdom, too. But for too long we've tended to think of that kingdom as primarily a future reality, rather than a present one. "Yes, we have our ticket to Heaven," we say. "And someday I'll be living in that spiritual dimension. But for now I'm stuck in this natural one."

This, of course, is not what the Bible reveals to us. The clear witness of Scripture from beginning to end is that we're living in both realms *now*. We just lost our capacity to perceive one of those realms back in the Garden. Only occasionally in the Old Testament did someone have the veil of blindness temporarily lifted, enabling them to glimpse the larger, fuller reality. For example, in 2 Kings 6, Elisha and his servant seem to be completely surrounded by a horde of hostile Arameans. The servant is panicked and cries, "Oh, my lord, what shall we do?"

> *"Don't be afraid," the prophet answered. "Those who are with us are more than those who are with them." And Elisha prayed,*

"O Lord, open his eyes so he may see." Then the Lord opened the servant's eyes, and he looked and saw the hills full of horses and chariots of fire all around Elisha. (2 Kings 6:16,17 NIV)

Living and functioning in the largely invisible spiritual realm is not a future prospect for the sweet by-and-by. It is a present reality and indeed a key part of our job description. It's central to our mandate to receive, contain and broadcast God's glory and presence in the visible realm.

So how does this bear upon the way we approach leadership in the Church? Well, because People of the Way simultaneously occupy two distinct but connected realms, we must recognize that the organizational elements we put in place in the material, visible dimension carry implications in the spiritual dimension. And vice-versa.

The question is, how can and should we go about trying to organize these very spider-y local manifestations of what is a very starfish-y global Church? And to what extent can and should we endeavor to make our local churches less like spiders and more like starfish?

First of all, it goes without saying that there is only one head of the (capital "C") Church. But once we get down here on the Earth it's perfectly legitimate to organize this thing called the Church. Organizations by necessity require ... well ... organization.

Moving a group of people from chaotic mob to loose affiliation and on to actual organization requires developing structures. And within that structure we must establish processes. Structure and processes are vital and necessary elements of any meaningful form of organizing. But this activity is not without a certain hazard. The danger is, the more structure we create and the more processes we implement, the greater the possibility that we will subtly shift from being God-sourced to being us-sourced.

We must be ever on guard against slipping into self-sourced-ness. That's why our definition of organization growth and change mustn't be:

> "WE MUST RECOGNIZE THAT THE ORGANIZATIONAL ELEMENTS WE PUT IN PLACE IN THE MATERIAL, VISIBLE DIMENSION CARRY IMPLICATIONS IN THE SPIRITUAL DIMENSION. AND VICE-VERSA."

- Getting more people to believe the correct things. (Doctrine focused)
- Getter more people to absorb more knowledge. (Education focused)
- Or getting more people to do better works. (Works or Mission focused)

One of the dangers we face is that in growth and developing leadership we often create methods and measures that are intended to aid in evaluation and strategy development. So leaders design metrics to help measure success, or need to improve. The danger inherent in this mindset is that anything that can be measured, by its very definition is something *measurable*. But what remains immeasurable are motives and source. If we are not careful we can wrongly gauge success or wrongly target strategies, because almost any measurable outcome can take place with or without God.

Somehow, we must continually pull back and keep our eyes, not simply on the outward circumstances, but we must also learn to look for heart, motive and source as the key targets of Kingdom movement.

Our focus ever and always must be on encouraging people to connect to Father-God as their Source rather then their own strength, knowledge, or efforts. Correct doctrine and knowledge and good works are wonderful and important. But they have to remain naturally occurring by-products and outgrowths of our vital God-connectedness—both individually and corporately.

As valuable as sound doctrine and Bible knowledge and good missional works are, we can't allow those things to define us. What defines us as being "the church"—People of the Way—is having been born of God and living "in Him."

> **"LIFE CREATES THE NEED FOR STRUCTURE. BUT STRUCTURE CAN NEVER GIVE LIFE."**

Nevertheless, as leaders, we will invariably find ourselves needing to create structure and processes in the organizations we lead—particularly when that organization involves people who are receiving, containing and broadcasting the Life of God. When the Life of God is flowing through an entity, growth and increase are the natural result. And that increase will demand new structures and new processes. As Jesus warned us, you can't pour new wine into an old wineskin unless you're prepared to find yourself standing in a puddle of wine with a ruptured leather bag in your hand.

We see a wonderful example of this principle in action with the fledgling Church in the book of Acts. The young church in Jerusalem, freshly connected to the Source following the Day of Pentecost, had the Life of God flowing through it and rapid growth was the inevitable result. That growth was straining the existing organizational wineskin to the breaking point. The opening verse of Acts, Chapter 6 tells us:

> *Now at this time while the disciples were increasing in number, a complaint arose on the part of the Hellenistic Jews against the native Hebrews, because their widows were being overlooked in the daily serving of food.*

Life produced growth, and growth created the need for some new structure and processes. So the Apostles spent some time in prayer and emerged with the concept of the office of *deacon*, and those deacons established some process to ensure that the distribution of food to the widows was equitable and efficient.

Now imagine some other religious organization on the other side of Jerusalem is jealously observing the early Christians as they multiply like crazy. They are the hot new thing in town. So they do a little investigating to find out what makes these "Way" people so special, and they learn that they have this structural office they call "deacon." So they naturally conclude that they need to establish the office of deacon so they can become successful, too.

Of course, the early church didn't grow rapidly because they invented the concept of deacons. They were inspired to come up with the concept of deacons because they were growing so rapidly. Life creates the need for structure. But structure can never give Life.

Still, on countless occasions I've watched churches try to emulate a structure, process or strategy that some other wildly successful church, corporation or movement has employed with the goal of replicating their results. And almost always the outcome is depressing. Most are spectacular failures.

First things first. As leaders we have to make sure that we, and those we endeavor to lead, are connected to the right Source. When that happens, you can be sure that Life is going to start bursting out all over the place, requiring that you think wisely and clearly about structure.

And whether the structures that emerge result in organizations that more resemble starfish or spiders, we will still face the dilemma that human organizations require positions with human authority. And historically mixing humans with authority has resulted in a volatile compound.

Thinking differently about leaders and authority—that's where we're headed next.

A PARABLE— PART VII

He had pushed down that nagging feeling for too long now. As a Master teacher, he had done everything he could think to bring to life this Game he had given his life to. Too many people walked out with a kind smile and a vapid handshake. Too many kind people said kind words and went right back to their kind lives.

Something wasn't right and he couldn't swallow the feeling any more.

Rather than sit in his office and prepare next weeks teaching, he began to walk. He walked out of his office and out to the edge of town. He heard the laughter and shouting of a group of people clearly having a great time.

As he drew near, he saw that a group of young people were playing The Game, right here on the edge of town, merely a half a mile from where he studied every week.

Standing and watching, he began to feel stirred. He had never actually played this Game, though he considered himself one of the top experts in their town. He watched

The Game unfold, inwardly noting mistakes or lapses on the field in front of him.

The play halted for a moment and one sweaty young man stepped off the field right next to him.

"Go in for me ..." he panted. "I need a breather."

And just that suddenly he was thrust onto the field.

Surrounded by boys a decade younger and with far less education, he tried to move into the play and was already left behind. This Game moved fast. Knowing what to do, he switched directions but The Game was already moving another direction.

One of his teammates came by and shouted, "Follow me this way!" With a grin on his face, he drew the Master Teacher in the direction of The Game.

But suddenly it came to him. His young teammate seemed to have known something he did not. He seemed to know where the ball would go, before it ever moved.

The Master felt like a student.

CHAPTER 9

AUTHORITY IN TWO REALMS

"The Universe knew we were coming."
—Freeman Dyson

"For though we walk in the flesh, we do not war according to the flesh, for the weapons of our warfare are not of the flesh, but divinely powerful for the destruction of fortresses."
—The Apostle Paul

The Four-Star General had complained of chest pains and numbness in his left arm, so, with some effort, he'd pulled on a jogging suit and his profoundly worried wife hastily drove him to the emergency room nearest their home in the Virginia suburbs of Washington, D.C. By the time they arrived and were ushered into an examining room, the General was feeling a little better. Panic was dissolving into embarrassment.

The ER nurse was all business and a model of efficiency.

"Take off your shirt."

"Have a seat up here."

"Relax your arm."

"Take a deep breath."

And with each crisply issued directive, the General grew more annoyed. It seemed the more the pressure in his chest abated, the less compliant a patient he became. You see, this man was accustomed to giving orders, not taking them. In his realm—the Pentagon—he wore a uniform that reflected his authority in that world. But there were no stars or medals on his jogging suit. On this night, it was the nurse wearing the uniform. He was in *her* realm. She barked the orders and he was expected to follow them. It made the General cranky. The forces at work in his body did not seem to recognize the authority afforded him in his day job.

We cannot have a serious discussion about leadership without spending some time examining the concept of *authority*. And our general's experience serves to illustrate an important truth about leadership in the Church. That is, authority in one realm doesn't necessarily translate into authority in another. And as I keep reminding us, we People of the Way are two-realm folks.

This is a truth our Professor of "The Game" ran directly into in our parable. He was accustomed to being authoritative in the classroom. He was the recognized "authority" about all the nuances of the rules of The Game. But the moment he got onto the field in an actual Game for the very first time, he discovered he had no functional authority at all. In the realm of theory he was a king. In the realm of practice, he was the lowest of the low.

When it comes to leading and organizing the local church, the challenge we face is that it is an entity with one foot very much in the natural world. As we've observed, it is the natural world that feels the most real because it is constantly bombarding our five senses. This creates a dilemma, in that human organizations require positions with human authority. However, the human-natural realm isn't the only one in play. The church has a foot in the spiritual world, too. It is a spiritual entity comprised of two-realm people with spiritual citizenship.

Authority in the natural world is well understood. We have presidents, chairmen of the board, CEOs, ship's captains, Army captains, police captains, team captains, and so on. In all of these cases, authority flows from the holding of a particular position in an organizational hierarchy. And that position usually was earned by displaying certain *natural* gifts and abilities.

Similarly, in the organization called "church," we have—depending upon the denominational tradition—pastors, elders, board members (not to be confused with bored members), deacons and bishops. The question is, what kinds of abilities and gifts did the people holding those positions display in order to gain them? Were they natural gifts or spiritual gifts? Or some combination of both?

You see, there is a thing called *spiritual* authority. In the invisible realm this authority is just as real and just as meaningful as is natural authority in the natural realm. In an ideal world, a person's authority in the natural realm—usually reflected in a position or title in the hierarchical structure of the church—will be paralleled by a similar level of authority in the spiritual realm. This is often not the case, however. Allow me to explain.

As I mentioned in the chapter called "Change the Right Thing," churches often promote to leadership people who are really good at Earth stuff. But being good at Earth stuff doesn't necessarily translate into being good at Heaven stuff. In many churches, the governing body of the church—usually the board of "elders" or "deacons"—is comprised entirely of men who have been highly successful in the realm of business or in a profession. Often these individuals are some of the wealthiest in the congregation.

I am not suggesting that this is necessarily a problem. Many of the most materially successful people I know are also some of the most spiritually gifted. But I have also seen churches place successful people in positions of authority for the wrong reasons.

Some pastors and church leaders follow the natural logic that a person's demonstrated skill at running a business organization will automatically translate into the sphere of church governance. They put a banker on the board to bring financial expertise; a real estate lawyer to add building and land acquisition savvy; a wildly successful entrepreneur to offer rapid organizational growth strategies; and so on. Others simply reason that giving a wealthy member a greater voice in the affairs of the church will prompt that individual to keep giving generously or perhaps even loosen the purse strings even more. This rarely ends well. It is how the bane of many pastors' existences—the "deacon-possessed church"—comes to be.

Again, natural authority and spiritual authority are two different things. To be a spiritual leader we must come to know the difference. Both matter, but the ability to discern between the two is crucial to be able to genuinely lead people in the Way.

Notice that when Jesus chose His senior team, He chose people who lacked human authority. I believe that He wanted to be absolutely certain that this crew did not assume that their human authority was why they were called to be His followers.

The distinction between human authority and spiritual authority is crucial. Spiritual authority simply means that someone has the ability to make an impact in the spiritual realm. Let me illustrate.

When a person walks into a room, and without any natural knowledge can tell that the other person in the room is angry, or sad, or happy, what is that? Those emotions are not physiological or chemical so that they actually occupy physical space. Something in the room is affected though, with enough impact that others can feel it. The reason people have the ability to impact the atmosphere of a room like that is because we have been created with the ability to take dominion.

A failure to recognize this can also affect the way growing churches structure their internal staffs. As a church expands, layers of hierarchy develop. A type of "corporate ladder" emerges. And given the way most of us humans are wired, if you put a ladder in front us, we are suddenly possessed with an overwhelming urge to climb it. Who among us doesn't enjoy a little more money, a little more status, a little more recognition, or being acknowledged as having done a good job? And in the overwhelming majority of churches and Christian organizations, salary, status, recognition and acknowledgement are tightly tied to the boxes on the organizational chart.

Don't get me wrong. Growing organizations need hierarchy and structure. But in any human organization in which hierarchy and structure have emerged, the people within that hierarchy will desire positions and authority. Why? Because, in part, that's precisely how we were created. When God set the first Man and the first Woman in the Garden, He vested them with authority and gave them a mandate for increase and expanding dominion.

So, while it is true that we were made for authority and dominion, not everyone carries the same preparedness to operate in authority or to exercise dominion. And herein lies the danger. Because cultivating spiritual authority often takes time and diligence, leaders are often tempted to make compromises or look for shortcuts. In other words, because our Four Star General is so impressive and credentialed in his "natural" domain—the Pentagon—it might be tempting for the hospital administrator to put him in charge of the ER. Of course, that would be a profoundly bad idea. The general hasn't put in the time or developed the skills necessary to exercise meaningful authority in the hospital realm.

Do you see it? As church leaders we need to endeavor to make sure the people we appoint, anoint, hire, and promote have congruent levels of authority in both the natural and spiritual realms. Yes, natural aptitudes, skills, and experience are important considerations when promoting someone in your organization or inviting a new person onto your elder board. But even more important are their spiritual credentials. And don't mistake morality for spirituality. To be sure, character and virtue are relevant, but there are lots of morally upright people who don't have a clue about spiritual things. Put another way, some people are just good at hanging out on the sunny side of the Tree of the Knowledge of Good and Evil, but they don't regularly eat of the Tree of Life.

We should aim to find, promote and develop leaders who have congruence and symmetry in both their natural and spiritual levels of authority.

How many times have we seen the following scenario? A famous actor, athlete or celebrity entertainer has an encounter with Jesus Christ and is born again. Immediately, those of us in the Church are so excited about our new high profile convert—our validating prize—that we immediately thrust them into the forefront of ministry. We do this in spite of the specific warnings Paul gave us about putting new believers into positions of ministry too early. It rarely ends well, for either the young believer or the cause of Christ.

Paul knew what we too often forget—that it takes time to grow in spiritual authority. So over and again we promote people beyond the appropriate level based solely upon what they can do in the natural realm. It is not possible to fake spiritual authority. But leaders who attain their positions solely through demonstrated natural ability will turn around and hire or promote on the same basis—indeed they are inherently incapable of doing it any other way. It is a self-reinforcing system. Earth-realm people recognize and value other people who are good at Earth stuff.

Remember Samuel's search for Israel's Next Top King? He was directed to Jesse's house and asked to see his sons. Jesse lined them all up for the prophet's inspection—all but one. He didn't bother to bring in David, the runt of the litter ... the least naturally impressive of all his boys. "Surely, if Israel's next king is a member of my household," Jesse reasoned, "he is one of these tall, handsome, charismatic, natural-born leaders here in my living room." But he wasn't. Samuel had to inform Jesse that God doesn't look for leaders the way we tend to. *"Man looks at the outward appearance but God looks on the heart"* (I Samuel 6:7).

You will recall that the only reason Israel was in the market for a new king in the first place was that Saul was failing miserably. The Bible explicitly tells us that Saul was a case of great-looking "natural" ability but all the wrong stuff on the inside. He was tall and handsome (I Samuel 9:2) but he was "little in his own eyes" (I Samuel 15:17). This pathological insecurity and a resultant inability to trust God under pressure became his undoing. Saul was big on the outside but small on the inside. I've known many amazing leaders who were just the opposite—unimposing to natural eyes but a formidable giant killer on the inside.

When, as with Saul, there is a severe asymmetry between natural ability and spiritual maturity, we see a specific destructive pattern commonly emerge. People good at Earth stuff but immature in spiritual things often resort to manipulation and maneuvering in their quest to gain promotion or opportunities. This is dangerous because it is impossible to manipulate others without, at some level, engaging the very kingdom we are commissioned to defeat.

When we attempt to lead a spiritual thing with only natural tools, it is seductively easy to mistake raw power for genuine authority. As Parker Palmer reminds us in his book, *A Hidden Wholeness*:

> The authority a leader needs is not the same as power. Power comes to anyone that controls the tools of coercion, which range from grades to guns. But authority comes only to those who are granted it by others. And what leads us to grant someone authority? The word itself contains a clue: we grant authority to people we perceive as "Authoring" their own words and actions, people who do not speak from a script or behave in preprogrammed ways. In other words, we grant authority to people we perceive as living undivided lives.[1]

King Saul's use of shortcuts (usurping the role of the priesthood by personally offering sacrifices), Machiavellian intrigue (attempting to arrange David's demise by sending him out to harvest Philistine body parts in order to win his daughter as a prize), and brute force power plays (trying to pin David to a wall with a spear) were all symptoms of a leader who has forfeited all real authority and has nothing left but Earthly power.

Don't misunderstand. Power isn't irrelevant. Power isn't meaningless. But it's not the same thing as authority. And it certainly isn't the same thing as spiritual authority. A drunk in the middle of an intersection waving a gun has power but no authority. An unarmed beat cop in that intersection has authority but limited power, whereas an armed police officer has both in balance.

Please remember, Jesus' mission was the re-integration of the realms of Heaven and Earth—an integration that was lost in the Fall. If we are going to be the kind of leaders who develop the kind of leaders who have congruent authority in both realms of existence, it is vital that we be all about what Jesus was all about. Also remember that our deceptively simple, three-fold assignment is to receive, contain and broadcast the Light and Life of God by connecting to Him (rather than our selves) as our Source. At the end,

---

1 Palmer, Parker J. *A Hidden Wholeness: The Journey Toward an Undivided Life*. San Francisco: Jossey-Bass, 2009.

King Saul had nothing in his leadership tool bag except human-sourced implements of manipulation, intimidation, and coercion. Thus he had nothing to contain or broadcast but fallen, human darkness.

EMBRACING FOOLISHNESS

Do you recall my quasi-historical illustration in the Introduction to this book—the one about the two generals and their competing strategies for conquering Jericho? If you skipped those opening pages, please go back and read that section now. It is very short and it holds the powerful insight that represents the organizing theme of this book.

That theme is that being a leader in the kingdom—leading people in the Way—means perceiving, responding to, and navigating a realm that is unseen but actually more real and more significant than the realm we access with our fallen five senses. You'll recall in that opening illustration, one general presented a logical, sensible strategy for conquering our hypothetical "Jericho"—a strategy firmly grounded in conventional wisdom and the known laws of physics. The other general presented a strategy that was handed down directly from Heaven. To natural eyes and ears, that strategy seemed like utter madness. But in reality, it was actually more logical, more sensible, and more grounded in the immutable laws of the universe then the competing approach.

> "WHEN WE ATTEMPT TO LEAD A SPIRITUAL THING WITH ONLY NATURAL TOOLS, IT IS SEDUCTIVELY EASY TO MISTAKE RAW POWER FOR GENUINE AUTHORITY."

The Heavenly wisdom strategy took into account a wider, more comprehensive set of "facts" than the Earth-wisdom strategy. Nevertheless, it appeared to be absurd to anyone operating from the narrower, more limited perception of what is "real." To use the Bible's term, it sounded like "foolishness." This is the language Paul uses in First Corinthians chapter 2 when he talks about how it is possible for us People of the Way to know "the mind of the Spirit" and "God's deep secrets." He describes how "natural" people can't comprehend or perceive these things. And how Heavenly strategies and approaches appear to be foolishness to them. Paul concludes that discourse by saying, *But we understand these things for we have the mind of Christ"* (v. 16, NLT).

To be a spiritual leader means embracing foolishness (or what appears to be foolishness to Earth-bound people). That is not to say that as leaders we should concoct the most absurd approach we can think of and label it "spiritual." But being a spiritual leader does require a willingness to apply unorthodox—occasionally wildly unorthodox—solutions to organizational challenges.

Would you agree that Jesus was and is a spiritual leader? Of course, He is the most fully spiritual leader the world has ever known. Well, His entire ministry was an exercise in flouting conventional wisdom and perplexing observers.

On one occasion His solution for a blind man in need was to spit on the ground and make mud. On another, He responded to the news that a dear friend was gravely ill by loitering around doing nothing until the man died. *Then* He marched off to go help. On yet another He responded to a call to feed a multitude by commandeering a young boy's brown bag lunch. He spoke to people He shouldn't have spoken to and ignored people who shouldn't be ignored. He hand selected protégés with all the wrong credentials.

Some bystanders of the day sincerely thought He was crazy. Fortunately, Jesus was once asked to explain His mode of operation and leadership. He essentially said, *"I only do those things I see My Father doing; and only say those things I hear My Father saying"* (John 5:19). In other words, Jesus explicitly stated that He was operating in two realms. He declared that He perceived a broader spectrum of "reality" than fallen men are able to perceive, and that His strategies were built upon Heaven-wisdom rather than Earth-wisdom.

A *spiritual* leader is a leader who understands that we live in a world that is both visible and invisible and that we stand with one foot on either side of that line. In Second Corinthians 10, Paul tells us (paraphrasing here): "Although we walk on the planet, we're fighting battles in the Heavenlies." This is the kind of military leader who will walk up to his king and recommend a city-conquering strategy that involved marching in circles and blowing trumpets.

If all we're doing is deploying the latest Earth wisdom and the hottest new corporate guru's Earth strategies we're going to end up taking six months and seven days to conquer a city (if we conquer it at all) instead of accomplishing it in a week! What is worse, taking that approach serves to enhance our reliance on our own natural abilities and convince us (falsely) of the superiority of our own wisdom. How dangerous is that? Worst of all, following that path causes us to miss out on the presence of God. We miss the joy, fulfillment, and thrill that come from being connected to the right Source.

You will also recall the other illustration I presented in the Introduction.

Making an important point with an absurd example, I asked how much sense it would make to impart the ten greatest, most insightful, leadership principles ever devised to a herd of lemmings. (Is a group of lemmings a herd? A pack? A gang?) The point was that when leaders operate from faulty assumptions they merely become more effective at pointing people in the wrong direction. As with our lemming friends, those directions are usually self-destructive.

This points to the danger of looking solely or even primarily to the corporate world and to the latest hot management guru for our methods and paradigms for organizing the church. The typical pastor's bookshelves sag under the weight of tomes dispensing the latest management paradigms and clever organizational metaphors. But the best leadership lessons in the world will do more harm than good if we don't recognize the two-realm nature of Christian existence. If we don't teach those we lead the difference between the visible and invisible worlds, and the relationship between the two, we simply become more efficient at getting to the edge of the precipice.

AUTHORITY AND SUBMISSION

As important as it is to understand that authority exists in two different but interconnected realms, it is equally vital to grasp that authority comes in different flavors; or put another way, that authority flows from different sources.

What authority has commonly come to mean over the years is essentially the ability certain people have to rule over other people in the natural realm. This common view has the unfortunate effect of infusing our approach to authority with fear and the expectation of judgment.

"Uh oh, there's a policeman. And I'm driving too fast."

"Oh no, I've just been called into the principal's office."

"Oh my, my boss wants to talk to me."

This familiar fear-and-judgment-laden experience is actually attached to only one variety of authority—namely *human* authority at its most basic level. This is the Earthly, very human phenomenon that we see wherever one person holds the ability to affect—for good or for ill—the life of another. In the workplace, a boss can fire you or give you a raise. In the classroom, the teacher can pass or fail you. In the military, the commanding officer can have you promoted or busted down to private (or simply assign you to cleaning toilets with a toothbrush for the foreseeable future).

As a manager or supervisor of employees at a large and ever-growing church, I hold some of this type of authority. But my hope is that this lowest and most basic type isn't the only flavor of authority I'm wielding as a manager. Hopefully I have much more than fear and the prospect of consequences in my leadership toolkit. If I'm operating in congruence with kingdom principles and kingdom values, then my authority increasingly comes from my ability to influence rather than any inherent power to threaten. But both types of authority are essentially human or natural in nature.

In other words, any unsaved person with a title can operate in fear-and-consequence-based leadership. Nor do you need to be a person of the Way to expand your authority by cultivating influence in the lives of those you lead. Non-spiritual people do this all the time.

Any time we contemplate the concept of authority, a companion concept invariably pops up. Wherever the topic of authority goes, *submission* cannot be far behind. In our hyper-individualistic, post-modern, authority-phobic culture, submission has almost become a swear word. But this stems from a misunderstanding of what true submission really is. Most people today mistake submission for *subjection*. The former is voluntary. The latter is forced. We give our submission freely, but subjection is imposed through implied or applied power.

We experience that squirt of adrenaline in the bloodstream when we top the hill in our cars and see a police car parked on the shoulder because submission feels like something other than what it really is. Subjection is the counterpart to "I can fire you." Or, "I could take good things away from you and do bad things."

> **"IF WE'RE OPERATING FROM A DISTORTED OR FAULTY DEFINITION OF SUBMISSION WE CAN EASILY HAVE A DISTORTED RELATIONSHIP TO THE AUTHORITIES."**

Submission and subjection are not the same thing at all. Submission means I choose to recognize and embrace another's authority. Subjection, along with its close relative, subjugation, involves force or the imminent threat of force. You're operating in submission to the policeman's authority when you dutifully pull over, accept the traffic citation, and then pay the fine. You would experience a heaping helping of subjection if you were to flee the police officer and then end up being dragged out of your vehicle, forced to the ground and handcuffed.

When I speak of authority in the context of kingdom leadership, I will always have this distinction in view. The reason this is important is that true submission is one of the keys to operating in spiritual authority. If we're operating from a distorted or faulty definition of submission we can easily have a distorted relationship to the authorities (natural and spiritual) around us. This invariably will hobble us—and them.

In the Kingdom we all simultaneously have authority and operate *under* authority. Jesus spent quite a bit of time trying to help His disciples move away from subjection thinking and into a submission mindset. He reminded them that it is the gentiles (those who don't have any understanding of God or His ways) who "lord it over each other" when they have authority.

I find it significant that the most impressed Jesus ever was with an individual during His ministry was when He encountered a Roman Centurion seeking healing for a beloved servant. Jesus, true to form, offered to accompany the Roman officer to his residence, but He got a remarkable response. The Centurion said, (paraphrasing): "You don't need to come. All you have to do is say the word. I know this because I too am a man under authority and also have people under my authority."

This man instantly recognized something about Jesus that he understood very well. Namely, that Jesus *had* authority and was *under* authority (in submission to His Heavenly Father). The Centurion understood something most modern believers do not— that these two aspects are related and inseparable. In other words, in the Kingdom of God only people who are under authority can effectively exercise authority.

POSITIONAL VERSUS RELATIONAL AUTHORITY

Human authority, at its best level, has more to do with a leader's ability to influence others to go in the direction the leader wants to go (relational authority) than in his or her ability to punish or reward (positional authority). This is an outcome one leadership expert calls "getting everyone in your boat rowing in the same direction."

Here is an example from my own experience. The department I oversee has several layers of organizational hierarchy, and I regularly lead departmental meetings in which individuals from all of these layers are present. In these meetings it has always been my goal to try to bring us to a place of consensus as a department. My goal is not to walk in and tell people what to do and walk out. Rather, my objective is to lead us to agreement about our direction so we can all move in unity. This is a very intentional strategy because I have learned there is a spiritual power in unity.

Please understand, I'm not taking this approach because it happens to be the one most natural to my temperament or because it is my preferred style as a leader. I do it because I am convinced that when we come into spiritual unity we tap into spiritual power.

As they say on the infomercials, "But wait, there's more!" In applying this approach consistently over the years I've discovered something wonderful. When you take the time and go to the effort to lead through *relational* authority, the time will come when those you lead will gladly trust you enough to welcome your *positional* authority. Allow me to illustrate.

A few years ago I was sitting in one of these departmental meetings and for some reason we were having trouble reaching a consensus about an approach to a certain problem. I was applying all my time-tested consensus building ninja skills honed in countless sessions as a marriage counselor. I used to joke that after my years helping couples on the verge of divorce I could build consensus out of oil and water. But not this day. Finally, one of the team members in the room spoke up and said, "Hey, Bob. We trust you."

I said, "What do you mean?"

"We trust you. Tell us what to do and we'll follow," she explained. There were nods of agreement all over the room.

It was a surprising new thought to me, and a fabulous gift from my team. What it said to me was that at some point my authority had moved from positional to relational authority—and that I had established a deep enough reservoir of relational equity that I could lead my team effectively even when consensus wasn't possible. In other words, we could be in unity even when we weren't in agreement.

You can appreciate how powerful this is when you remember what we examined earlier about the power of our actions to empower one or the other of the two kingdoms. If I use fear, threat and the intimidating authority of my position to get people to go my way—if I haven't fostered trust and buy-in within the people I'm trying to lead—I may get some short-term results but I have actually empowered the wrong kingdom in the process. Control-and-command leadership fosters subjection, not willing submission. *I must do what you say because you have the power to make my life miserable.* Sadly, many people in Christian organizations are living and working under that mode of leadership.

I believe that style of leadership almost always empowers the kingdom of darkness. Why? It doesn't allow people the freedom to choose. The kingdom of God is a "whosoever will" kingdom. The King of the Universe always gives us the opportunity to "choose this day" whom we will serve. When you lead solely out of positional authority, you may have people's bodies but you don't have their hearts. In that moment when my staff said, "Hey Bob, just make a decision and we'll run with it, even if we disagree with you," there was no fear of negative repercussions behind that willingness. It wasn't, "We'll go along because we're afraid you'll remember this when it is time for our next annual review." It was, "We trust you, therefore we give ourselves to you." Do you hear the difference?

NATURAL VERSUS SPIRITUAL AUTHORITY

Jesus is on trial. He stands before Pontius Pilate, a local governmental ruler for the Roman occupation who is questioning Jesus but getting no response. Finally an exasperated Pilate asks, "Don't you know I have authority over your life?" Pause that, and rewind to a graveyard near Bethany a few days earlier. Jesus is standing outside the tomb of a dear friend. Here He speaks. Actually He *commands*, "Lazarus, come forth!"

It is important to realize that the Man who was asked, "Don't you know I have authority over your life?" was He who has authority over death. Ironic, yes? Jump forward once more to Jesus before Pilate and push "Play." We hear Jesus telling the bewildered governor that real authority doesn't come from where he thinks it does. Indeed, that it comes from a place Pilate can't perceive with his five senses. An invisible realm.

> "PILATE UNDERSTOOD HUMAN AUTHORITY IN ITS RAWEST, MOST COERCIVE FORM. BUT HE WAS CLUELESS ABOUT SPIRITUAL AUTHORITY."

Pilate understood human authority well. He knew it in its rawest, most coercive form. But he was clueless about spiritual authority.

Through the exercise of spiritual authority we can bring life from God, to us, and through us into the natural realm. We can bring power from God, to us, and through us. We can bring love, joy, peace, patience, kindness and all those good things from God, to us, and through us. Remember, we are two realm people with a foot in each realm. At any given moment, we can transform the atmosphere in a room. We can transform a sick body. We can transform a sick relationship. We can bring positive, transformative change to things simply by stepping into them and exerting the authoritative force that is in us because of our connection to God. Spiritual authority is about reshaping the natural realm by bringing the spiritual realm into it. Through the application of spiritual authority, the supernatural realm takes dominion over the natural realm.

We have to stop thinking about authority solely in terms of position. It's vital that we start thinking about influence across the full spectrum of reality—both visible and invisible. In the visible realm the exercise of authority involves leading people to become themselves and to give of themselves in a common cause. And in the invisible spiritual realm it's about affecting the atmosphere of the places in which you have authority. One of the key things to realize about authority on the spiritual side is that you don't have to be physically present to have influence.

I've observed that so much of the atmosphere of a local church or organization flows outward from the person that leads it. His or her spiritual authority radiates throughout the organization. And this takes place whether the leader is standing in front of the staff or congregation or ministering on the other side of the world somewhere. That influence isn't dependent upon proximity to be felt.

That flow of *anointing* (to use a perfectly good old-school word) is from the head downward. As leaders, whatever is in us flows *from* us.

Here is a key implication of this understanding that spiritual authority transcends time, space, and what our five senses can perceive. There is a significant difference between employment and spiritual covering. Covering is like an umbrella of protection. Employment is merely a legal status. Employment means you get a paycheck and whatever benefits are stipulated in the employment agreement. Having a leadership covering means far more. It means having somebody standing in a place of authority who makes a way for you to be who you were meant to be. It means being a part of something bigger than yourself—and having something beyond yourself flowing to you and through you.

THE LIMITS OF POSITIONAL AUTHORITY

For many, one reality of being a part of a large organization is finding yourself in the middle of the organizational chart. By definition, the nature of positional authority is that your authority can really only flow one direction on that chart—downward. Positional authority has very pronounced limits. Not so with relational authority. This type of authority can flow laterally and upward through an organization.

A popular concept in business circles these days is "leading from the middle." It's an important idea. But the only way this is possible is through the cultivation of relational authority. It is possible to lead those who are above you on the org chart. And by the same token, it can be appropriate to receive leadership from someone who is positionally beneath you. Remember, submission is not about subjection. And also recall the lesson of the Roman Centurion—you can only exercise authority if you're willing to be in submission to authority.

For example, some of the most spiritually authoritative people in the organization in which I work throw away trash every day. That's not a metaphor. I'm literally saying that some of our facilities maintenance people are very spiritually mature and wield a large amount of spiritual authority—even though their names would appear near the bottom of our official org chart. And if I'm the kind of leader who is secure in who he is in Jesus Christ and understands spiritual authority, I'll recognize there are wonderful, important things that I can receive from them. But only if I practice submission to authority.

At the same time, if I'm too prideful or status-conscious to open myself to receiving from such a person, I'll miss out on something unique and helpful from God. That doesn't mean I let just anyone tell me how to do my job. But if someone positionally subordinate to me sees something that I don't see, or has a perspective that I don't yet have, and I am not willing to receive that from him, I've made myself and everybody under me poorer. In other words, I can fail fundamentally as a leader precisely because I'm too concerned about control and status.

Conversely, it's equally possible that a person with one of the most prestigious titles in an organization may be one of the least spiritually mature. Even so, we commonly assume that the higher you look on the Christian organizational ladder, the more spiritual maturity you'll find. In reality, you may just find people who are good at climbing ladders. In fact, sometimes the striving and driving that often accompanies insecurity can propel people to pursue positions and authority. And sometimes manipulation actually works.

That uncomfortable admission leads us naturally to the next stop in this examination of authority—what I call *counterfeit* authority.

CHAPTER 10

AUTHORITY: COUNTERFEITED, HIJACKED & ABUSED

"If you end your training now — if you choose the quick and easy path as Vader did — you will become an agent of evil."
—Yoda

"Of all tyrannies, a tyranny sincerely exercised for the good of its victims may be the most oppressive."
—C. S. Lewis, God in the Dock: Essays on Theology

Gríma Wormtongue. There's a lovely and evocative name for you. When a reader of J.R.R. Tolkien's *Lord of the Rings* epic fantasy novel encounters that name for the first time, there is little doubt as to the character's status as good guy or bad guy. If you saw the trilogy of films based on Tolkien's novel, you will remember Wormtongue as the slimy, manipulative advisor who had bewitched King Théoden of Rohan. The Wikipedia entry for this character tells us that, "Gríma serves as an archetypal sycophant, flatterer, liar, and manipulator."

In the films, the nature and effects of Wormtongue's influence are blatantly clear. His appearance is as slimy as his name suggests. His controlling influence over the king is obvious as well. Under the spell of his advisor, the once strong and vigorous Théoden gradually becomes ashen, feeble, and even has cloudy cataracts over his eyes (he can no longer see or perceive reality accurately). Wormtongue manipulatively whispers in the king's ear to bring about policies that are harmful to the kingdom but in line with Wormtongue's selfish ambitions.

This fantastical scene is obviously fictional, but it depicts a phenomenon that is very real—especially if you pull back the limiting veil of our natural senses and see with spiritual eyes. The fact is, wherever you find real authority—natural or spiritual—you will invariably have people who try to attach themselves to the one who possesses that authority in order to gain influence. Such a person finds a way to wield influence without having to shoulder the corresponding responsibility. That's why I call this "counterfeit authority." As any legitimate leader knows, authentic authority always comes with responsibility. Indeed, the carrying out of responsibilities is what authority is for.

Nevertheless, the successful authority "leecher" has the best of both worlds. He or she can steer policy and outcomes toward his or her preferred agenda but without carrying the burdens of responsibility or accountability. All of that remains on the one with authentic authority.

In the *Lord of the Rings* movie, even a child can easily discern the insidious nature of this dynamic. It is obvious that a schemer has parasitically attached himself to a person of power in order to advance his own agenda. The manipulator is creepy looking. The negative effects on the legitimate authority are obvious. In real-life organizations and churches however, something similar takes place all the time—but it is far subtler in appearance and therefore harder to perceive.

In most cases the authority hijacker doesn't appear to be wicked at all. On the contrary. He or she often looks like the model employee or volunteer. Such a person will consistently do what I call over-function. He shows up early and stays late. She will obsessively seek control and try to micro-manage. This person is seemingly everywhere.

As I pointed out in the previous chapter, sometimes you will see this behavior when a person's natural authority isn't paired with a commensurate and symmetrical level of *spiritual* authority compelling him or her to over-function in order to make up for the deficit. But in other cases this hyper-activity is driven by Wormtongue-ish compulsion to hijack legitimate authority.

Sometimes this over-functioning manifests as micromanagement.

Sometimes it's 100-hour workweeks. Sometimes it's flattery and effusive affirmation of the legitimate leader's wisdom and insight.

The Bible holds numerous examples of would-be Wormtongues—each one attempting to hijack authentic authority in order to pursue their own selfish agendas. But one Bible character in particular is so identified with this insidious infiltration of leadership, her very name has come to be synonymous with it.

THE JEZEBEL SPIRIT

Her husband's name was Ahab. More than 850 years before the birth of Christ Ahab rose to the throne of Israel as the rightful ruler of the northern kingdom. His reign began with great promise. There were military conquests, the securing of borders, not to mention the rising economic prosperity that tends to accompany these things.

> **"AS ANY LEGITIMATE LEADER KNOWS, AUTHENTIC AUTHORITY ALWAYS COMES WITH RESPONSIBILITY. INDEED, THE CARRYING OUT OF RESPONSIBILITIES IS WHAT AUTHORITY IS FOR."**

But then there was the fateful decision—in raw defiance of God's explicit instructions to the kings of Israel— to forge an alliance with Ethbaal, pagan king of neighboring Tyre and Sidon, by taking his daughter in marriage. The Greek historian Menander tells us that before becoming king, Ethbaal was a priest of the demonic goddess Astarte (Ishtar). This means his daughter, Jezebel, was raised from birth in the blood-soaked sensuality of pagan temples.

Thus an idol-worshipping priestess of demonic deities became queen of Israel. As the king's wife, she had no legitimate authority to make policy in the kingdom. Her role, as with previous queens in Israel and Judah, was to give the king an heir and remain quietly in the background. But Jezebel coveted Ahab's authority. She had ambitions and agendas she wanted to advance.

Unable to gain legitimate authority, she sought the next best thing— influence. She had no organizational power so she cultivated indirect control instead. She manipulated her weak-willed husband and steered the nation on an idolatrous course that would ultimately result in the northern kingdom's destruction and the disappearance of the ten northern tribes from the timeline of history. To this day we refer to these tribes as "lost."

Working in and through the person of Jezebel was a very real, very insidious animating demonic spirit. Here in the New Covenant era, armed with post-Pentecost powers of discernment and spiritual insight, it is possible to see that the "Jezebel spirit" is still very much in business. Of course, in the popular culture's vernacular, a "Jezebel" is a euphemism for a seductive woman with an agenda. But the fact is, the Jezebel spirit is an equal opportunity employer (and destroyer). It will eagerly use either a male or a female host to carry out its work—attaching itself to, and hijacking, authentic authority.

Before exploring some ways this spirit attacks Christian leaders, allow me to offer a word of caution. Prudent awareness that individuals in an organization can be operating under the influence of a Jezebel spirit is wise, but watchfulness can gradually mutate into a witch-hunt if we're not careful. Vigilance can metastasize into paranoia. I've seen it happen and it can be hurtful.

Even so, the damage caused by this over-reaction is nothing compared to the carnage inflicted daily upon good Christian organizations via individuals under the influence of the same spirit that animated Jezebel. Sometimes it's a person who comes into an organization and tells a leader, "I can really help you and make things easier for you. Let me take some of this load off of you. I'm great at this thing that you struggle with." For a leader of a growing organization who might occasionally feel overwhelmed, such an offer can feel like a lifeline.

A leader who is not functioning fully in balanced, symmetrical authority will be tempted to say, "Okay, you're it!"

Anytime we set up a human hierarchy where people are in charge of people, invariably someone in that organization will feel they deserve more of something (recognition, affirmation, money, visibility, responsibility) than he or she is getting. How that person responds to that feeling reveals much about that person—his or her character, spiritual maturity, spiritual authority and understanding of how God's kingdom functions.

Every person ever brave or foolish enough to be the coach of a kids' sports team has seen this phenomenon in the form of a dad who believes his kid deserves more playing time or a bigger role on the team.

People employ all kinds of strategies to remedy this perceived injustice. When those strategies are purely human (rooted in the natural realm) we call it manipulation. But sometimes this activity also has a dark non-natural component—the Jezebel spirit. The sole objective of this spirit is to attack the *prophetic* and *revelatory* mission of the church. By "prophetic" I mean our role as People of the Way to help the lost and un-fathered hear the voice of Father-God. And by "revelatory" I mean that part of our mission that involves introducing His supernatural presence and power into this natural realm.

When a frustrated individual under the influence of a Jezebel spirit is denied the control they seek through natural promotion, they will instead work on their attachment to the person who does hold the power they seek. They build alliances within the organization in a quest for counterfeit authority. The part of this that can be seen and perceived with human senses is only the tip of the iceberg. Or to deploy a different metaphor, a small tree with a huge underground root system. Hidden beneath the surface of all this seemingly wholesome and praiseworthy activity is an orchestrated, Trojan Horse assault upon the plans and purposes of God.

Think about it. If a stronghold can take root in a human soul, it can also take root in an organization. If you and I can open a door to Satan through a choice we make, an organizational leader can certainly do the same.

Satan can and does look for the people within a team who are the least connected and most prone to turn on others. He can relentlessly whittle away at the connecting cords of relationship. What a sobering thing to realize that the space between us can empower the kingdom of darkness. We keep the enemy from gaining a destructive foothold in the organizations we lead when we stay close to God and to each other.

When someone with a Jezebel spirit seeks to hijack a leader's authority, he or she will invariably seek two things: to become indispensible to that leader, and to exploit (and if necessary create) relational conflict within the team.

What does someone with this spirit in full-blown manifestation look like? The answer depends entirely on where you are in the organizational chart.

As I've already suggested, if you're a leader whose authority is being hijacked, this person may look like a model staff member or volunteer—at least for a while. This person needs to be indispensible, so he or she is often the most productive person on your team. I've discovered that with many people who end up being used in this way, there is often deep rejection in their past that needs to be healed. In an effort to address that wound, they tap into an anointing that isn't from the Kingdom of God.

But if you happen to find yourself working under this person, your perception will be starkly different. You will most likely see wrath, manipulation, control and intimidation on a regular basis. When you are above this person on the org chart, they have a powerful need to win you over.

And what if you're a peer of such a person? Which of these facets you see will be determined by how you are perceived by them. If that person sees you as someone who will buy into their authority, they will be your best friend and will try to manipulate you into allying with their proposals and positions. If they sense you are immune to their charms and deceits (witchcraft, actually), they will look to box you out or, if possible, get you removed from your position in the organization.

What should you do if you discern that you have such a person embedded in your organization? The length and scope of the book doesn't permit a comprehensive answer to that question. For that I recommend John Paul Jackson's book *Unmasking the Jezebel Spirit* and Bill Johnson's teaching series titled *Leading from the Heart*.

The short answer is this: rooting out a Jezebel spirit requires the bringing to light of something that is hidden. In particular, it requires the eyes of the leader whose authority is being hijacked to be opened to something that he or she currently does not perceive. This is a spiritual problem (we wrestle not against flesh and blood), and therefore prayer and fasting are significant parts of bringing to light that which needs to be illuminated. Ultimately the complete, restorative solution depends upon the person in authority seeing what he or she doesn't see. Why? Because it takes the right level of spiritual and organizational authority to root out this problem.

If the person being used in this destructive way is your peer or above you on the organizational chart, then your primary recourse is to pray. Pray for the legitimate authorities who are under attack. Pray for discernment and against deception. If you are organizationally below this person, direct confrontation can rebound and make you look like a troublemaker.

The temptation can be to fight manipulation with

"THE SOLE OBJECTIVE OF THIS SPIRIT IS TO ATTACK THE PROPHETIC AND REVELATORY MISSION OF THE CHURCH."

manipulation—scheming with scheming. This trap *must* be avoided. It is possible to come under the influence of the same spirit if we try to engage it in our own power and with carnal weapons. For example, stealthily building your own network and alliances to counter those of the Jezebel will merely exacerbate the very divisions the enemy is trying to create. No, we defeat the spirit of darkness by introducing light. As much as it depends on you, be at peace with all men (Romans 12:18). Be rightly related from your heart and the heart of God. The person operating under that spirit will wilt in the face of love after a while, though at first he or she may seem to be taking advantage of it. Build relationships based on love and trust, not manipulation.

Truth telling, honesty, submission to authority, prayer and fasting are our weapons against the Jezebel spirit. And they are mighty in the pulling down of strongholds.

OTHER AUTHORITY TRAPS

Facing an attempted hijacking isn't the only pitfall faced by those called to lead and steward authority in the Kingdom of Light. A deceptive attack by a Jezebel is an outward threat. However, some of the pitfalls kingdom leaders face are inward. As with most things in the Christian life, the most consistent battlefield is within our own souls. Here are just a few of the traps inherent to the pursuit and stewardship of natural authority:

1. **THE DRIFT INTO SELFISHNESS**

    There is nothing wrong with having a desire to lead. Indeed, anyone God has called into leadership will almost certainly carry some sort of inward desire to influence and organize others in the advancement of God's kingdom plans and purposes. Nevertheless, it is not uncommon for this very wholesome impulse to gradually, subtly morph over time into something less healthy—something more self-serving.

    As we see in the journey of a spiritual leader, no leader makes his way into a position and influence without paying a price. That price may merely be time and effort. Or it could be paid in the form of the endurance of hardships such as rejection and mistreatment. No matter what the currency, persevering in the path of leadership exacts a toll.

    In fact, along this road it is possible to experience a perfect storm—a confluence of two factors—which can constitute a deadly and influence killing trap.

    The first of these is the common assumption that leadership is accompanied by privilege. Whether it be a better parking space, more influence, or tickets to major sporting events, we have all seen that an increase in status can open the door to an increase in opportunities and benefits. Again, this is not inherently wrong; it just sets up some wrong expectations. As soon as these privileges become expected entitlements, the spiritual leader is on the verge of seduction. The seduction is to make a subtle shift in the heart that says, my position now places me above others, and I should reap the benefits.

The trap lies in the word *should*. You very well *may* reap benefits from holding a position of leadership. Indeed such "perks" are likely to come. But the moment your heart begins to believe that you're entitled to them—that you should have them—you have begun to forge a perilous attachment to comfort and to the realm of the visible.

The second part of that trap is the thought process that says, "I have paid a price, therefore I deserve ..."

When the presumption of a right to privilege and the thought, "I am deserving because I did good," converges in our souls as leaders, we draw an invisible line in our hearts. The dangerous line demarcates "us" and "them." This trap is insidiously easy to fall into when you're on the ascending path of spiritual leadership. To maintain a kingdom leadership mindset, we must take note of how Jesus navigated this part of the journey.

The special privilege that Jesus held onto was the assertion that His disciples did not know the cup He was about to drink from, and He was reserving the task of crucifixion for Himself and no other. The point is not to make us all martyrs. It is simply to keep us aware that the incidental privileges of leadership—the perks, the praise and the visibility—must be held with an open hand. They cannot be allowed to become our aim or our entitlement if we are to continue being facilitators of bringing God's Kingdom into our reality.

2. "GIVE US A KING" SYNDROME

The danger in this pitfall lies on both sides of the equation. Leaders and followers alike can fall into this group dynamic.

We see it both in the triumphal entry where Jesus is thrust by the crowd into a premature position of visibility, but we see it much more clearly in the story of Israel asking Samuel for a king in 1 Samuel 8.

In this account we see Israel asking God through the prophet Samuel to give them a king to rule over them. It is a penchant in the human race to desire someone to rule over them. From the difficulty of serving a God who is quite Invisible and can therefore sometimes seem unavailable, to the discomfort that many humans have with taking personal responsibility, something about most people calls out, directly or indirectly, for someone else to rule over them.

Israel calls out to God, asking that He would appoint a king over them. Whatever the drive behind this, at least two elements of the story are worth noting. Even more, they are worth caution lest we fall into the exact same trap.

First we see that God gives them a significant warning that involves the repeated word "take." He tells the people that if He gives them a king, the king will *take* from them. This is followed by a long list of all that will be taken. Everything from family members to land, wealth, and legacy falls in this list of things that will be taken if they allow a monarch to rule over them. The loss we face when we let others stand between us and a personal experience of God is that we lose significant elements of our life and livelihood.

Second, and even more chilling is this simple realization: God tells the people that it is a bad idea, but He will do it if they continue to ask.

What? God will give us something He recommends against?

This is important to know. Too often we think that if things are going well, it implies God's blessing. In this case, the whole "king" thing comes to pass, but not only is God not in favor of it, He has sternly warned against it.

Leadership in His Kingdom must never be a way that we give away, or take from others, the freedom producing responsibility that each person has for their own relationship with God.

We must not let others thrust us into a place of being their "king," nor should we so enjoy the donkey ride that we begin to bask in and enjoy a position that God has not yet smiled upon.

3. THE NUMBERS TRAP

When you have a message you're passionate about, it's natural to want more people to hear it. I've never met a preacher or teacher who wasn't convinced that if having 200 people in the seats was a good thing, having 400 would be even better. And there's nothing wrong with feeling that way. Leaders have a God-given desire to lead. And as we observed about the "Give us a King" Syndrome above, having a message that helps people and an anointing to deliver it does indeed tend to draw a crowd. But therein lies the pitfall.

The bigger the crowds grow, the greater the temptation to compromise to keep them coming. When numbers move from being a happy byproduct of carrying out your kingdom mission to being the mission itself, you've fallen into this trap. And it happens all the time because it's subtle and gradual.

4. PROMOTION ADDICTION

When you're operating in your gifting and in full connection to God as your Source, success just happens organically. Fruit and growth and increase spring forth out of that connection. But it's easy to start feeling the expectations of others as a weight to perform. Soon you're feeling real pressure to replicate that success. If you're not vigilant, you'll find yourself frantically repeating what worked in the past but doing so without the connection to the Source that produced the success in the first place. You end up pursuing the applause of men rather than the face of God.

Let me say again, there is nothing inherently wrong or improper for a leader to design and desire growth, promotion or increased impact in his or her sphere of calling. But it is possible to become so intoxicated by promotion for promotion's sake, that you are no longer endeavoring to serve people but rather to *please* them. Little compromises can accumulate as you progress higher and higher though the ranks of an organization until they comprise a complete abandonment of your true calling. Inch by inch you can move away from the people you are called to help, and toward the people who are best able to help you. Of course, every little compromise and concession to expediency can be rationalized.

5. MISSION AMNESIA

Furthermore, as promotion happens, we can incrementally move away from the core things to which we're truly called. Of course, we are first and foremost called to be sons and daughters of God, and to love our brothers and sisters. As we do this effectively in a Christian organization, it is inevitable that we will be asked to take on new responsibilities. We will receive recognition and promotion. It is at this point that we can begin to serve the thing we're doing instead of being served by it. Doing "ministry" for a living means we have to do it even if we don't feel like it, because we're getting a paycheck for it.

In a similar way, the more authority we obtain, the more we are able to get things done "for God." Again, the danger is that we can begin to pursue authority for authority's sake. Instead of letting God pull us upward organically, we can begin intentionally building a machine designed to get us to the next level.

6. INSULATION AND ELITISM

As self-sourced growth and promotion separate us from the people we're called to be connected to, it becomes very easy to say we don't have the energy or time to give to people because of the demands of the position. Some leaders build elaborate structures around themselves, creating a buffer between themselves and all the people clamoring for time and attention.

Yes, there will always be excessively needy people who are essentially black holes for time and attention. Nevertheless, there is a very real danger in thinking, "I've graduated to a level at which I don't have to get my hands dirty anymore." We can begin to long for a more sterile brand of ministry. But please remember, *sterile* carries two meanings. It can mean both the absence of dirt *and* the inability to produce life. If we ever get so far up a hierarchy that we're no longer willing to be a normal person among a normal people, then we need to reevaluate.

Authority, by definition, is a powerful thing. This is why knowing that it can be counterfeited, hijacked, abused, and misapplied is vital for every leader of people of the Way. It takes a special kind of leader to stay connected and grounded in the midst of growth and promotion. It takes a *spiritual* leader. And one doesn't become one of those overnight. Spiritual leaders walk a path. They undertake a journey.

Examining that journey is our next point of exploration.

A PARABLE—
PART VIII

The next day he was sore. Terribly sore, and terribly alive. He knew The Game in a whole new way. Nothing he had learned in school had prepared him for the speed of The Game, and the seemingly unpredictable things that could happen in the flow of play.

And nothing he had learned in school had told him what playing The Game would do for his soul. He was exhilarated and exhausted, and could think of very little except the next time he might be able to play.

He had discovered things about himself out there on the field, and his body struggled to catch up. He knew he could work through the soreness and fatigue, but he was hungry to get out there again with others and let The Game work its power in him.

Just through the one time alone, he realized how essential the team was, and how the design of The Game forced them into an amazing synergy. He realized what you could never learn from the sidelines: The Game could actually teach itself. In the flow, and on a team, learning … just happened.

But he could also tell that this was a beginning. So much more than "learning" could happen. Life and Joy could happen.

What on Earth would his friends think?

CHAPTER 11

THE JOURNEY OF A SPIRITUAL LEADER

"People don't take trips. Trips take people."
—John Steinbeck, Travels with Charley: In Search of America

"Do not follow where the path may lead, go instead where there is no path and leave a trail."
—Ralph Waldo Emerson

"Dr. Livingston, I presume?"

Missionary David Livingstone arrived in Africa in 1840 with two goals: to explore the continent and to end the slave trade. In England, his writings and lectures ignited the public's imagination regarding the "Dark Continent" and elevated Livingstone to the status of a national hero.

In 1864 Livingstone returned to Africa and mounted an expedition through the central portion of the continent with the objective of discovering the source of the Nile River. As months stretched into years, little was heard from the explorer. Rumors spread that Livingstone was being held captive, lost or dead. Newspapers headlined the question "Where is Livingstone?" while the public clamored for information on the whereabouts of their national hero. By 1871, the ruckus had crossed to the shores of America and inspired George Bennett, publisher of the *New York Herald*, to commission newspaper reporter Henry Stanley to find Livingstone.

Leading an expedition of approximately 200 men, Stanley headed into the interior from the eastern shore of Africa on March 21, 1871. He led his party 700 miles on foot through burning salt plains, swamps and impossibly dense rain forests for 236 days before he found Livingstone in Ujiji, a small village on the shore of Lake Tanganyika on November 10, 1871.

Stanley began his journey an obscure American reporter who had grown up a wandering orphan. He ended it a world famous adventure icon and the utterer of one of the most famous phrases in the English language.

> **"THE PEOPLE AROUND YOU WANT SOMETHING THAT THEY THINK COMES FROM YOU, WHEN IT ACTUALLY IS JUST COMING THROUGH YOU."**

Every journey has a beginning point. But to be a truly epic journey, the destination must lie far away from the point of origin, and the path must hold numerous pitfalls, hazards and tests. This journey does more than test the traveler; it transforms him or her. The journey to becoming a spiritual leader is just such a journey. Truly epic.

Now, anyone who is an authentic leader in the Kingdom—wielding both natural and spiritual authority—didn't get to that place in a day. It was a process. A journey. And although each spiritual leader's journey is unique, I have discovered that most of these adventures have some common waypoints. In this chapter we'll explore these commonalities and expose some of the traps and pitfalls that can waylay emerging spiritual leaders.

BEGINNINGS

Very few of us start out thinking that leadership in the Kingdom is our destination. We just—start. We have a transformative encounter with God. We become Fathered. Often the most noteworthy aspect at this stage of growth is gratitude coupled with a desire to express it. We want the people we care most about to experience what we have experienced. Almost by definition the journey of a spiritual leader begins not as a quest for influence and responsibility, but simply as an organic expression of joy at being a son or daughter in the family of God.

Our arrival into the family of God is often marked with an awareness that we have arrived here not out of our own effort or merit, but simply by having received a free, undeserved gift. We come into the Kingdom not in order to serve, but because we become aware that Jesus has served us. We receive. Gratitude naturally flows from our hearts. We worship because we see God's goodness. We connect because we need the flow of God's Presence.

In many cases it is this natural spontaneous response to God's gift that results in our first foray into leadership—quite by accident. We're excited and freshly connected to the right Source. We don't think about it. We just *are*. Those around us are impacted as the life and light of God flows through us. Others follow. It's as if when Jesus is elevated in our lives, He draws men to Himself. We do little or nothing and people around us are affected by our connection to God. So more people are drawn in.

One day we stop, look around, and realize to our surprise that we're a "leader."

That is a perilous moment. It is at that instant we can first become aware of the expectations of others. It becomes harder to just *be*. Our brains and egos get involved. If we're not vigilant, we can easily move from living out of a natural overflow of connectedness to the Source, to being driven by the expectations and affirmations of others or our circumstances.

The people around you want something that they think comes *from* you, when it actually is just coming *through* you. They are looking for something that used to come naturally, but they begin asking for, either directly or indirectly, that which used to be a natural outflow. Subtly, gradually, certain shifts occur. We go:

From responding naturally to God, to trying to please people.

From responding to overflow, to trying to produce.

From spontaneity to expectation.

From waiting on God, to trying to perform on demand.

The net effect of these shifts is that we go from living with God as our Source to self as source. Here is how that phenomenon manifested in my own journey as a spiritual leader.

Early in my life as a believer I was teaching what now seems like a relatively small class, but back then I thought it was a quite a crowd. I had begun by teaching directly out of the overflow of my own relationship with God. I would fellowship with the Father during the week. At some point during that fellowship He would show me something cool or life-giving, and I would share it with the group on the following Sunday. What I taught grew organically and spontaneously out of my connection to my Father. People who came to the class were blessed and helped. They told others about it and the class grew. And because the group kept growing, I eventually began to feel a creeping sense of pressure. I started feeling this increasing weight of other's expectations.

I found myself thinking, "Oh wow, a lot of people will be there next Sunday. They've been told I'll have something really great to say. I need to make this good!" In other words, I started feeling pressure to produce mechanically what had previously been occurring organically. What began as a simple act of receiving, containing and broadcasting the life of God gradually metastasized into ... *performance.*

Something very similar happens early in the journeys of many spiritual leaders. You can, if you're not mindful, turn your attention away from the very thing that began producing fruit in your life in the first place. You can gradually let the pressure to perform and the desire to meet expectations take over. You'll start "helping" the Spirit of God.

Sometimes this shift is so subtle and incremental, you're not even aware it's taking place. You just subtly start to think you've reached the limit of what God can do. Or perhaps you get fearful that He won't show up and do what He's done in the past. For whatever reason, you decide, "I'd better take over now." Or you simply start to feel the weight of responsibility and the pressure to deliver something that you've delivered in the past.

If we're not careful, we cease allowing God to be our source. We neglect the Tree of Life and instead turn to our own knowledge of good. A teacher will start to feel the weight of needing to bring some insight no one has ever encountered before. A manager will feel the need to develop a new process. A builder will start feeling the need to breathe life into something out of themselves instead of something that came to themselves. A visionary will succumb to pressure to deliver something new and fresh so people will get excited.

Obviously the manifestation of this trap varies with the calling, but in every case a perceived or imagined pressure starts to build in the mind of the emerging leader. And if he or she isn't careful, the response will be to subtly move to self-reliance (self-sourced-ness). Once this begins, it sets us up for another dangerous drift.

A FAMILY OR A JOB?

Is ministry a family function or a job? Are we good shepherds or hired hands? Are we adopted or merely employed?

Don't misunderstand. There is nothing wrong with getting paid for doing work in ministry. The workman is worth his wage, and I am a solid believer in paying people for their time, effort, skills and gifts. The real question is motive.

Here's a common track for volunteers in ministry. We've already seen that when you operate in your calling within an organization in consistent connectedness to God as your source, it's natural and predictable that people are going to notice. New assignments are going to come your way. You'll be given more responsibility. You may even be offered a job. (Or *not* offered a job when you had begun to anticipate that you would be.) Those are both interesting moments—ones that are fraught with soul-peril.

The moment we begin to attach value to our roles, whether it be financial, recognition, relational validation, or positions and titles, we begin to bring all of our humanity right back into the midst of what was previously a free-flowing stream of God's Spirit. Suddenly, certain questions become vitally important: Who gets to speak? Who gets to play the guitar? Sing the lead solo? Who gets credit? Who gets the high profile assignment? All of these (usually unspoken) questions can begin to infiltrate the once-pure motives of a person's heart—especially after becoming a "professional."

Once again, the manifestations vary widely, but the root remains the same—a subtle but progressive shift away from dependence on and connectedness to God and toward self-sufficiency. This shift invariably creates the opportunity for the untended knots in our souls to be exposed. Recognizing and responding to these knots is a crucial part of the ongoing life of a spiritual leader.

This part of the journey tests our motives. And at no time are our motives tested more rigorously than when we encounter rejection or disappointment. As we're about to discover, this is actually an essential part of the journey.

DEALING WITH REJECTION AND DISAPPOINTMENT

One of the most common features of the journey to spiritual leadership is a universally painful—and often devastating—experience. The process of growing into spiritual leadership at any level, in any capacity, brings us face to face with what seems to be the most common and potentially dangerous obstacle along the path to leadership: *rejection*.

The fact is, I've never encountered a mature spiritual leader who hasn't had a soul-searing encounter with rejection along the way.

I've broached this subject on numerous occasions as I've spoken to groups of pastors and leaders. Invariably, as I speak, I'll see in my listeners' eyes flashes of recognition, of identification, and of remembrance. Sometimes I see tears. Indeed, any time I speak publicly to a group of leaders about the issue of rejection, it seems I tap into a deep vein of truth, relevance and pain for them. For leaders, rejection is clearly a widespread and potentially paralyzing human experience.

A painful stop in the valley of rejection is more than just a near-universal experience for emerging spiritual leaders; it is a formidable force to be reckoned with. Every time I bring up the topic in a presentation, I can feel the atmosphere shift in the room. I can see in the faces of men and women an immediate and visceral response to the word *rejection*. For most, the word connects to some very significant moment or season in their lives.

Developing leaders of every type and stripe invariably confront moments of disappointment and frustration. These are fork-in-the-road moments. How they are handled—whether well or badly—will carry major implications going forward on the journey. For leaders of the Way, rejection—and often from a surprising source—seems to be an almost universal rite of passage.

We see this reality reflected repeatedly in the Bible. Moses' first attempt at leading an Israelite uprising when he killed the Egyptian slave master was met with a rejection so complete that he ended up fleeing Egypt and spending the next 40 years as a sheep herder. Even after his miracle-studded return to Egypt he experienced initial rejection of his demands. Later his wife rejected him; when forced to circumcise their sons, she seems to have taken the boys back to Midian with her. Ultimately Moses is reunited with his sons but there is no indication in scripture that Zipporah ever rejoined Moses. Ultimately he experienced a heart-wrenching betrayal by his brother Aaron and the elders of Israel when they slipped into idolatrous golden calf worship when he was away meeting with God.

Rejection. Disappointment.

The deliverer Samson was betrayed by his own wife. Young David, a loyal and valuable servant to King Saul, spent years fleeing the king's jealous, irrational, murderous wrath. And the King of Kings was despised and forsaken of men. He is *"the stone that the builders rejected"* (Psalm 118:22; Acts 4:11).

Clearly here, I am not referring to the kind of frustration that comes from getting insufficient recognition, or being overlooked for a special role or position. While these things can be disappointing and even painful, I am really talking about something much deeper.

Ironically, this rejection often happens during or immediately after a season of pursuing the Lord and His Presence. In many cases it comes as a direct consequence of choosing to do some things that are right and good. In such moments, people or groups who have been family or even friends may suddenly turn on us. In some cases this turning feels like an outright betrayal. Often it comes from family or spiritual family—someone who has been a father or mother figure to us—mentors, elders, or those in whom we have trusted the most.

I believe this is such a consistent and significant experience that it is worth exploring a bit further.

A long time ago, in a galaxy far far away, I found myself in a situation I could never have dreamed. In the confidentiality of my private practice days I was handed information about a leader whom I loved a great deal, and one whom my entire family received from.

This information indicated that he was in serious trouble and headed for a fall. Because of the way the information came to me, I could not approach him directly, nor did I have the kind of relationship with him that would allow me to push him into talking about what was going on in the secret places of his heart and life.

> "I DO NOT BELIEVE GOD LIKES PAIN. NEVERTHELESS, I AM CONVINCED HE NEVER WASTES IT."

I tried every way I knew to make myself available and invite him to talk, to no avail. Finally, the family member who had shared with me decided to have a confrontation, and as the counselor, I accompanied them in this confrontation. What followed was one of the most painful seasons I have ever endured.

A man I loved and served under, in his own quest for self-protection, began to campaign against my family and me. As a result ultimately I ended up being forced out of roles where I had labored to build relationships and touch lives. Along the journey many wounds, accusations and broken relationships littered the path. The church I had loved became the vice that closed in on me.

In the midst of all this, I had a dream. This dream—combined with some key teaching I heard during that painful experience—probably kept me from walking away from ministry altogether. Not only did these particular truths keep me in ministry, they got my feet back on the ground. They kept my mind anchored in sanity during what seemed like one of the most insane periods of my life.

In this dream, I was standing in front of a young man I had been meeting with for several years. He and I were simply talking, standing in a barn. I glanced away for a moment and when I looked back, the young man had hung himself.

The height and position of his body required that I place my shoulder under him and lift so that I could remove the chain from his neck and release him from his self-inflicted demise. As I hefted his weight on my shoulder, I reached up over his shoulders and loosed the chains. As I did, the full weight of his body fell into my arms, and his unconscious, gray face fell against my chest.

Forgive the graphic description, but as he fell into my arms, he vomited all over me. Here is the odd part. Everywhere that his vomit contacted my body, I felt an electrical charge surge through me. So strong was this "electrical" sensation that it woke me—yet the sense of electrical power continued to surge through my body and hands.

This night would mark a dramatic shift in my own experience of God's active Presence in my teaching and ministry. All I mean by this is that from that day forward I saw more real impact on real life circumstances in the things I taught and did.

You see, that teaching I referenced a moment ago equipped me with one vitally important truth to sustain me in that season. I had heard a Bible teacher named Jack Deere make a statement along these lines: "When we are rejected or wounded, and we respond with genuine love, the power of God is released on the Earth, through us. We can choose to love in the face of pain and rejection."

I do not believe God likes pain. Nevertheless, I am convinced He never wastes it. If we think of the single act that most released God's Power in the Earth, a completely innocent man was both rejected and executed, and responded with nothing but love. In the face of the strongest weapon formed against Him, Jesus responded with the most potent weapon ever leveled at the kingdom of darkness.

Love in the face of rejection.

My friend in the dream was dying by his own hand. His mortal wound was self-inflicted. At personal cost to myself, I bore the burden of his body to release him, and saved him from falling to the ground. Rather than thank me, he vomited all over me. In the face of his worst I gave him my sacrifice—and power was released.

Love in the face of rejection. It is easy to love and broadcast God's Nature in the face of kudos, kindness and kindred-ness. We might even be able to muster up our own love in such a setting. But when we choose love in the face of rejection, God is empowered *in* us.

As I weathered my first personal storm of rejection, I discovered something in me that I did not realize was there. One day I said to myself, "I really thought that if I started to learn to do the things that Jesus did, people would really like me, not reject me." The first problem with that thought, as I eventually realized, is that this approach didn't even work well for Jesus Himself. He was really good at doing the things Jesus did (the best ever!), and it got Him not only rejected, but executed. Why would I expect anything different?

As I turned my attention to these thoughts I discovered a very important thing taking place in my soul. You see, before I came to know and follow Jesus I had been a bit of a loner--wanting people to like me, but too shy to really pursue many friendships.

As I began my own journey of growth as a spiritual leader I found that people *did* like me. People responded and people gathered. They said nice things about my teaching and it felt great! As I came to the close of the season of rejection I discovered something massively important. I discovered that a significant idol in my own heart was dying a slow, agonizing death. I had no idea until then that I had served the idol of people pleasing.

There may be no greater trap for a growing leader than to worship at the altar of people pleasing. Rejection, as painful as it is, swings right at the root of this vine. Weather a season of rejection while choosing love and you will find that your need for the accolades of others is significantly reduced.

This trap of chronic people pleasing could spring on us once the size of the crowds we're drawing begins to swell. Immunizing us against this trap is a key benefit of having walked through the valley of rejection. The people-pleasing trap can be disarmed and rendered harmless by enduring a season of painful rejection. This allows us to remain safely and solidly on the journey. Christ is formed in us in a powerful way even when—or especially when—we choose to die to our need for the approval of others.

When we face seasons of rejection we also face a fork in the road. We can choose the path of love in the face of pain, or we can choose to allow our own untended souls to rise up and become our protection. In fact, our protective mechanisms can cause us to reject and hurt others. We actually become spreaders of the disease that has damaged us.

Furthermore, when we return hurt for hurt, an eye for an eye, we find ourselves in the ancient and tragic deception of believing we are serving one Kingdom, while we're actually empowering the enemy's kingdom. This is the very trap this book was conceived to warn against.

Now that we have identified some key pitfalls on the spiritual leader's epic journey, let's move on to an exploration of some of the values that emerge and are cultivated along the way.

CHAPTER 12

THE VALUES OF A SPIRITUAL LEADER

"For what shall we do when we wake one day to find we have lost touch with our heart and with it the very refuge where God's presence resides?"
—John Eldredge, The Sacred Romance

"For what you see and hear depends a good deal on where you are standing. It also depends on what sort of person you are."
—C.S. Lewis, The Magician's Nephew

Because spiritual leaders have eyes in two realms—natural and spiritual—their guiding values flow from that dual perspective. Rather than live by mere rules and man-manufactured guidelines, a supernatural perspective informs the actions and reactions of a spiritual leader. In the same way that night vision goggles guide a "special ops" soldier after dark—allowing him to see what others cannot—these values can guide a leader in the invisible spiritual realm. Values produce sight, and then sight guides actions. Those values, in no particular order, are:

1. A SPIRITUAL LEADER IS KINGDOM FOCUSED

More than any other guiding value this simple instruction from Jesus provides the most significant key for anyone who wants to live a spiritual life. The powerful truth of this idea is in Matthew 6:33: *"Seek first the kingdom of Heaven and His righteousness ... and all these things will be added to you."*

Underlying this is a simple yet profound principle. In fact, this principle empowers the remaining values on this list. Stated simply it is this: Whatever you seek first orders and organizes every other aspect of your life. This is a way to describe the power of focus and how it creates order in our lives, whether we recognize it or intentionally use it or not.

We seek a variety of things in life, but we all have something that we seek *first*. Seeking first refers to the priority we give something we consider most important. It's not a religious idea, it is the instinct of humans with appetites. At one level, for many Americans the target of "seek first" is caffeine. Our daily routines reveal that we prioritize a trip to the coffee pot, or in many cases, our preferred coffee shop. We joke about what we are like before our morning coffee. We're only half-joking when we use "I haven't had my coffee yet" as an all-purpose excuse.

> **"WHATEVER YOU SEEK FIRST ORDERS AND ORGANIZES EVERY OTHER ASPECT OF YOUR LIFE."**

Because we seek our caffeine first, other aspects of our day and routine are ordered or organized around that target. Food, clothing, these things may all be put in second and third place around that which is in first place.

Similarly, if we seek first the attention of other people, we by default give the humans in our orbit authority to organize many other aspects of our lives. If we seek first financial security, our money has been given dominion over our time, thoughts and habits. And so it goes. Anything we seek first has been given the power to organize our thoughts, emotions and focus.

Living a life of seeking first the Kingdom is important for two reasons. At the most basic level, it is necessary to do this in order to live a spiritual life. But it is absolutely vital to exercising any level of spiritual leadership. Why? Because anything at all that you seek first carries the power to rule, order, and organize every other aspect of your life.

Sadly, a misunderstanding of this principle works against even the most well-meaning prospective leaders, because it results in succumbing to some very ancient temptations. By "temptations" I do not necessarily mean sins. I am referring to those things that appear to be *"pleasing to the sight and desirable to make one wise"* (Genesis 3:6).

Health and life in a growing church or ministry will produce a variety of signs. The Presence of God commonly results in things like increased attendance, more activity, public attention and a higher community profile, and so on. As a result, it's tempting for leaders to look upon a "successful" church, take note of what they are doing, and "seek first" to replicate those results. Mistaking effect for cause, we seek first attendance, activity, visibility or any other common Christian goal.

If we fall for this reversal, we will put all our efforts into trying to produce effects or outcomes. Our desire for more of the *evidence* of God may inadvertently produce less of God Himself.

If seeking first the Kingdom of God is the most important value (and it is, hence the term "first"), it would follow that we must define the Kingdom as something *seek-able* and *findable*. Here's my simple working definition:

> The Kingdom of God is—God, present on the Earth, available and willing to operate in the present moment.

This definition makes Matthew 6:33 about where we put our attention, rather than about how hard we work at appropriate tasks. This is a vital aspect because all too often people misread this exhortation (*seek first the Kingdom*) as an admonishment to try harder at the assignment of Christianity.

Like the illustration used earlier, if you have ever fiddled with a malfunctioning electronic appliance or component, trying diligently with every adjustment you can imagine to get the darn thing to work, only to discover the thing isn't plugged in, then you can understand the principle. Regardless of the number or type of adjustments that you make in the component, without a connection to a power source, no adjustment is sufficient.

Seek first the power source, and all the adjustments will then be added to you. Simply put, the spiritual realm is the source of truth and power for the natural one. Seek first the Person and Presence of God, and He will spur growth, He will empower, He will guide, He will inform; He will adjust anything that is out of order.

The number one guiding value of a spiritual leader must be the seeking first of the Kingdom of Heaven and His righteousness—which results in leading others to do the same.

2. A SPIRITUAL LEADER LEADS OTHERS TO HEAR GOD

As I have contended throughout this book, it should be our goal to connect people to the Person of God, not the organizations and institutions of God. As the previous value on this list asserted, our number one core value must be to seek first the Kingdom of God. So what does that look like, practically speaking? What activity, more than any other, constitutes "seeking first?"

Before I answer this, let's remind ourselves of the way we have described the Designer's original purpose for the human soul: to receive, contain, and then broadcast God. This is a very different thing than *serving* God, or doing things *for* God. Anything properly ordered in the Kingdom has God as the Source. He is a big fan of being that Alpha thing. So when we set out to define an activity that would constitute "seeking first the Kingdom," we must be careful to not subtly shift the initiative back over to the human side of the equation.

With that cautionary note in place, I would say that the number one activity that allows people to "seek first the Kingdom" is listening for His Voice. Deuteronomy 8:3 tells us that God wants us to be people who live by every word that proceeds from His mouth. And true to our religious, Tree of the Knowledge of Good and Evil impulses, we tend to twist that clear statement into a mandate to memorize Bible verses and bear down harder in our efforts to obey them.

Receiving God—receiving His life—is as simple as tuning in to His Voice. Remember, faith always comes by hearing. Always has. Always will. And whatsoever is not of faith is sin. So the life that we are created to live—the process of seeking first God's Kingdom—is hearing. Hearing God speak.

It is important to keep in mind that the God of the Bible is not necessarily in the advice giving business. When God speaks He is not trying to counsel, advise, or even cajole us into deciding to go along. When God speaks He is *creating*.

If God tells us about His plans, He is calling those plans into existence with the very words we are hearing. If God tells us about ourselves, He is creating (or re-creating) in us with those same words.

Hearing God is *the* action item that defines a spiritual leader. Just as important, leading others to hear God for themselves should be the primary activity of a spiritual leader. For too long we've been willing to hear and broadcast content ("This is what God said") instead of process ("You too can hear God speak") When we lead others to hear God for themselves, we are restoring a race of people to planet Earth who live by every Word that proceeds from the mouth of God. When leaders tell others only what God has told them, they create dependents.

As a marriage counselor, rule number one is to teach couples, in the moment, how to interact with each other. Allowing yourself to get "triangle-ed" into the relationship means you have become the go between. You hear the wife and communicate *for* her to the husband. Then you hear the husband and communicate *for* him to the wife. This is not only bad marriage counseling but it creates two distinct additional problems.

First, these couples will never actually learn the process of communicating with each other. They'll only learn how smart their counselor is (or is not). This actually makes the counseling process more about the counselor than the married couple. The goal of marriage counseling ought to be the success of the couple, not the reputation of the counselor.

The second pitfall is that this process makes the couple entirely dependent on the counselor. If they have not learned to communicate for themselves they will either call the counselor between sessions, or simply wait until the next weekly meeting to resolve their next issue.

If we are not careful, we can make this precise mistake and create these same problems in the people we lead. Imagine if people only heard God once a week and only from a trained professional. What a tragedy that would be. But isn't that precisely the situation in huge swaths of the Church today? Imagine if our children only heard from us what God *has* (past tense) said, but never learned to hear God for themselves today.

Spiritual leadership is simply marriage counseling between the Bride and the Bridegroom. We must get others to communicate directly with God, and learn how not to insert ourselves as the middleman.

> "WE LEADERS AREN'T COMMISSIONED TO TEACH PRINCIPLES SO FOLLOWERS CAN RUN OUT AND TRY TO APPLY THEM BY HUMAN EFFORT."

We can see the danger of the "middleman" role in a well-known story in the book of Exodus. God invites Moses to bring the rest of the people up to the top of the mountain where God and Moses have been spending quality time together. God has a clear intention that He expresses to His friend in Exodus 19:9. He says, "Behold, I will come to you in a thick cloud, so that the people may hear when I speak with you and may also believe in you forever."

God wants the people to hear Him speak. He wants them to hear *Him*. He does not want them to hear Moses' interpretation. Clearly, from His words, faith has and always will come from *hearing*. Now watch what happens.

As the story unfolds and Moses deals with the humanity of his people, he gives back to the people *his version* of what God said. Just a chapter later, in fear the people are asking Moses to hear *God for them*. Moses—meaning well, I assume—tells them why God wants them to hear for themselves. Listen to his words. Moses said to the people, *"Do not be afraid; for God has come in order to test you, and in order that the fear of Him may remain with you, so that you may not sin"* (Exodus 20:20).

In a single chapter, but through the filter of "second hand hearing", the message of God goes from "hear so you can believe and follow" to "hear so you will be afraid and not mess up."

We see a perfect example of the very thing God is trying to avoid. When people allow others to hear God for them as their primary channel of relationship instead of faith, the result is that we all hear through the filter of the designated "hearer."

We must lead people to hear for themselves, so they can believe forever and follow.

3. COMMUNION

Clichés become clichés for a reason. Something worth repeating tends to get repeated. If it's greatly worth repeating it gets repeated even more. Soon it can get repeated so often that it is repeated by people who don't even truly understand it. They say it because they've heard it said.

Such is the case with the oft-repeated axiom that spiritual leaders need regular, personal communion with God. It's true, of course. If one of our primary goals as a spiritual leader is to foster a connection for people in their own relationship with God, we must first make that connection a reality and a priority in our own lives. Remember, we leaders aren't commissioned to teach principles so followers can run out and try to apply them by human effort. Rather, our goal is to impart or transmit something that is contained in our souls to those around us.

My point is, if we give away that which is in us (and we do, whether we intend to or not), then we may actually give away something entirely different than we intend if we do not first practice communion with God before recommending it to others.

First we must understand that communion with God is not merely a set of "practices." Reading a Bible, reciting words in our minds (praying), stillness, singing songs—all these are practices we might associate with a personal conversation and connection to God. Yet any of these can be implemented without God's involvement.

As we saw in our examination of content versus process in Chapter 1, if we only teach these practices (content), and never really pass on the process of truly connecting to God, we only replicate lifelessness. But what if instead we pointed to these disciplines as nothing more than potential pathways to truly connecting to, hearing, and receiving from the God we worship?

Several years ago, I began to be aware that I was particularly dry— spiritually and emotionally (the two are connected). Around the same time I became aware that I had really not had a regular time of Bible reading or prayer for quite a while. Thinking I had properly diagnosed my problem, I made a fresh commitment (make that re-commitment) to go into my office early each day to spend some my time with my Father and in His Word.

On day one, I arrived and glanced at my desk. Spread out upon it were things that represented all the tasks and obligations awaiting me that day. They were calling to me. Taunting me. But with herculean effort I turned away from them, sat down with my Bible and began to read some words, and then recited some other words that sounded like prayers in my mind.

I had dutifully "prayed" and "spent time" in the Word. Nevertheless, I was keenly aware that I had made no dent at all in my sense of dryness. In fact, I felt I might even be a bit drier than when I had begun.

I decided I would remedy this problem by changing what I was doing. I read again, only more slowly, and I paused and reflected in between phrases and ideas. Doing this made it a bit harder to ignore the stack of papers on my desk, but I got all the way through a chapter this time. Success! Or ... not.

Recognizing that I felt no more connected than I had before, I started over again at the beginning of the chapter. Maybe I had missed some vital, invigorating truth. I was only three sentences in when an annoying stirring arose in my soul. After a moment, the stirring began to form words in my mind. I heard these words: "Bob, just put the book down and talk to Me." It was a life-changing moment.

Jesus admonished the Pharisees one day, saying, *You search the Scriptures, for in them you think you have eternal life; and these are they which testify of Me*" (John 5:39). In a very similar way, any of the practices that we might associate with a "good Christian's" devotional life can also become the very busy-ness that distracts us from engagement with God. This is a constant hazard if we do not recognize the distinct difference between devotional practices and true communion. If we leaders do not recognize the difference, we're just passing on requirements, disciplines and practices. And in so doing we will be teaching others a form of "godliness" that lacks the power of God's Presence.

Second, I think it is crucial to recognize that shame and guilt are never effective motivators for any true experience with God. If we are not experiencing meaningful communion with God personally while we are urging others to do so, our own hypocrisy accuses us internally. Unintentionally, our own shame can become the fuel for how we instruct others. Instead of handing them the richness of our own connection and allowing the fragrance of that to draw people into an appetite driven practice, we hand them a guilt-driven practice.

4. DISCIPLES NOT DEPENDENTS

Closely related to this practice of teaching others to hear and interact with God for themselves is understanding that we are trying to help people become disciples of Jesus, not dependents on humans or human systems.

When Jesus said, "I am with you always, even to the end of the age" (Matthew 28:20), He was not employing a metaphor. He was not telling us that He would be "with us" in the sense that He would be rooting us on. He meant exactly what He said. He is with us. If this is true then we can help people become His disciples by teaching them how to interact with Him.

> "WE ARE NOT TRYING TO LEAD PEOPLE INTO A PERFORMANCE BUT INTO A RELATIONSHIP, AND ULTIMATELY INTO A CONDITION."

Disciples are people who follow and become like the person they follow. They are not necessarily people who follow a prescribed path, or ascribe to a certain set of doctrines or practices. Disciples are people who literally follow and become like another person.

Again, it comes to this question: does the true gospel place the weight of bearing fruit and bringing about change on us—or on God? The core message of this book answers this question. Our connection to God naturally and spontaneously produces fruit apart from our own efforts or strivings.

5. PROCESS AND MOMENTS

Another significant skill and perspective for an effective spiritual leader is to help people really walk out the balance of believing in a God of powerful moments while teaching them the way to live life in between the powerful moments. Or how to recognize the seasons in which the divine goal is growth rather than immediate change. It is crucial to seek with whole-heartedness all that God has in any given moment, while also helping people to live with true faith when hope seems deferred.

Pressing into moments of encounter and asking God for big things at any given point is a vital part of leading people in relationship to the God who wants to give more than we can ask or imagine. At the same time, living life with and pastoring people who are teetering on the brink of disappointment with God and experiencing devastating life circumstances is just as important.

If we are going to believe and teach that God wants to be present and active with His people on the Earth, we should expect big things. We should be learning how to pray for the sick with authority and learning how to take dominion over creation. We should be learning how to partner with a God who is all-powerful. The great moments of God—whether they come as a result of Him being present and active in a worship service or in a street corner conversation—are crucial for validating many of the things that have already been proclaimed here in these pages.

But what of the one who is still sick? What do we do with those who don't experience the breakthrough or blessing they asked for? The child dies. The business fails. The ship sinks. The bad guy gets away with it. Tragedy unfolds undeterred, and in some cases seems to accelerate. What do we do with those circumstances? More importantly, what do we do with those people?

Powerful moments must occur in the context of process.

Living a life—and leading people toward a life—that is characterized by a day to day process of knowing and learning to trust God requires a willingness to stay right in the middle of some hard things. Not just to stay there, but to stay there and care. Even so, leading and caring doesn't necessarily mean being obligated to provide explanations.

One of the greatest temptations for leaders of any sort is to try to explain or defend God in hard moments. What is really needed most is not to *explain* God but to *contain* Him. To stay connected and present.

Comforting those who mourn, or weeping with those who weep is central to the nature of God, and therefore central to our representation of Him in this realm. I would add to that not just mourning; there is deep ministry in waiting with those who wait.

Sitting in a hospital room or a coffee shop with no answers but with tenacious love is a great spiritual discipline. Answers are usually a way that we make ourselves comfortable with other people's pain or process, and they seldom do much to truly help the people with whom we wait or mourn. Answers do not take away pain, and in some cases, the awkwardness with which they are offered can actually increase the pain or shame of someone in a hard situation.

We must lead people to seek the God of powerful moments, while still helping them live a day to day life that may be marked by seasons of discomfort, long periods of seemingly unanswered prayer, or lengthy stretches of unexciting but vital growing and maturing.

6. FREE PEOPLE FREE PEOPLE

A significant aspect of spiritual leadership is that we are not trying to lead people into a performance but into a relationship, and ultimately into a condition. This condition is not something that is achieved by striving or effort, it is something that springs naturally from proximity and connectedness.

Too often we see people mistakenly trying to lead people into conformity with expectations or into the rote performance of rituals. As we've seen, there is no life in these things and therefore no power.

Listen to the instructions Jesus gives His disciples in Matthew, chapter 10. Preparing to send them out into the countryside, He casually tells them to raise dead people back to life and to heal sick people. He tells them to engage the spiritual realm and send darkness fleeing. But it is His summary statement that is important in this part of the discussion. After telling them all this, He looks at them and adds, *"Freely you have received, freely give"* (v. 7).

Jesus tries to convey something very important here. Whatever is inside of you is what you give away. This makes the issue of tending to our souls and walking a path of transformation more important than any skill, education, training, or knowledge we might possess.

A highly educated person who contains anger will broadcast anger. A brilliant speaker who is laden with legalism will broadcast law. A credentialed counselor who is filled with pain or judgment has nothing to give away but pain and judgment.

This fact alone makes the way we know and tend the contents of our souls the most important aspect of preparation for spiritual leadership. If we contain anything but the life of Christ, all of our training simply makes us more effective at passing on anything but the life of Christ. Proactively, and really to the point, if we contain the life of Christ we give it away in whatever context or conversation we find ourselves in.

Life and Freedom. We receive. We contain. We broadcast. We cannot lead others into a place that we have not gone, or are not going.

7. VALUES BOTH MASCULINE AND FEMININE

The topic of women in leadership is a hot one in the church these days. In fact it's occasionally downright incendiary. Many churches are wrestling with questions about the roles women can and should play in leadership.

In the spirit of thinking differently and questioning long-established paradigms, I encourage you to approach these questions through the lens of some concepts put forth in LeeAnn Payne's groundbreaking book, *Crisis in Masculinity* (Baker, 1995). In it, Payne, the founder of Pastoral Care Ministries, wrote in spiritual, biblical terms about the true masculine and the true feminine. Her work did not focus only on men and women, but also on the aspects of God's nature that are expressed in masculinity and the equally divine aspects expressed in femininity.

In other words, God didn't draw from His own nature to build man-ness into the first Man but then pull woman-ness out of thin air when it came time to create Woman. Both the masculine and the feminine are different facets of the same multi-faceted God.

I believe this paradigm can provide a helpful context for thinking clearly and biblically about women in leadership roles. There is a pitfall, however. In fact, I believe we could actually make some positive changes that result in providing more opportunities for

> "GOD DIDN'T DRAW FROM HIS OWN NATURE TO BUILD MAN-NESS INTO THE FIRST MAN BUT THEN PULL WOMAN-NESS OUT OF THIN AIR WHEN IT CAME TIME TO CREATE WOMAN."

women to occupy leadership roles and still not actually address the more important issue. Allow me to explain.

In her book, LeeAnn Payne described the traits of the true masculine and feminine. Specifically she summed up the nature of each in a single word. For men, she said God's nature is most expressed through the male as *initiative*— the ability to start and originate things. In complement, she describes that the nature of God expressed through the true feminine is best summed up in the word *receive*.

Let's back up and look at the nature of God first, and then re-approach the male and female aspects of this. God describes Himself in several ways that demonstrate this complementary pairing. He is the Alpha *and* the Omega. He is the Author *and* the Finisher of our faith, the Beginning *and* the End.

These images display the two (in one) attributes of God that we see in the male and female. The "beginning" is a clear picture of initiative, and the "end" or completion, is a beautiful picture of receiving. This picture is even clearer as we define this word with more color. Specifically, the idea of receiving is not simply receiving the way one would a gift or a package. It has to do with receiving the way you would receive a person. Embracing. Making a place for them. Not merely a place, but a space where they are received, seen and valued, the way Grace receives a human in whatever condition they show up. This is the way soil receives a seed.

All of this explains why I prefer the word *nurture*. Soil nurtures a seed and makes a place where the life within can grow to fruition. Initiative, the masculine nature, is the planting of the seed. Nurture, the feminine counterpart, provides a place and a context where the seed can grow and come alive.

Think of God's Hebrew name, *El Shaddai*, meaning "the large nurturing one." This is a feminine name, and specifically refers to the nurture provided from a nursing mother. This is a significant part of the nature of God expressed in Eve. This is God's design for the feminine nature.

Get ready. This truth has implications. It suggests that we do more than just be more open to putting women in roles of leadership. I believe it reveals the need for true femininity in both men and women who are spiritual leaders. Now, hang with me here while I explain. I'm not suggesting that all spiritual leaders need to be androgynous metrosexuals—skinny jeans, manicured nails, hipster fake eyeglasses and all.

I am referring to a need to return *nurture*—the primary feminine trait—to a place of prominence in spiritual leadership.

Look at the picture Jesus paints for us in the parable of the soils. A man goes along the path sowing seed (initiating life). Jesus makes it clear that this seed is the Word of God. But the determining factor in outcomes is not how much seed was sown or how good it was. It was all good seed. The determining factor in growth was nurture. The kind of soil that received the seed was the key element of how much life resulted.

Picture a church culture in which a lot of programs are started, but not many mature disciples develop as a result. Seeds are being planted like crazy, but no fruit is forthcoming.

You are picturing a culture where nurture is lacking. You are picturing a culture where the milieu cannot support the type or amount of life being initiated. You are picturing a culture that is missing the contribution of the true feminine.

The issue is not simply about whether or not women can occupy certain roles in the church. It is about developing a culture where the Author of our faith also has the opportunity to be the Finisher of it. We need to examine whether or not we have removed the impact of the true feminine from its role in church leadership.

If Jesus came to give us life and life abundantly, what might be the result of that gift if the soil we have prepared cannot support the depth of the Life He has delivered?

Listen to the words of Paul as he describes his ministry to the Thessalonian church:

> *But we proved to be gentle among you, as a nursing mother tenderly cares for her own children. Having so fond an affection for you, we were well-pleased to impart to you not only the gospel of God but also our own lives, because you had become very dear to us. (I Thessalonians 2:7-8)*

Nurture—a feminine trait yet a significant attribute of God—can be found in both females and males. Paul seems to recognize that, for all they had initiated in this church, the people still needed "tender care" in order to bring to maturity that which his team had begun.

I fear that in a culture that has had primarily male leadership, we have lost the value of the true feminine as an essential component of spiritual leadership. Nurture, discernment and intuitive thinking are all elements that strengthen a two-realm leader. A strong dose of "being in touch with our feminine side" might bring us a strength we often fail to consider.

To a degree, we not only fail to consider this strength, but in any culture that becomes too "male-centric" we can actually begin to view these attributes as weaknesses to be eliminated from the equation. Thus, even when women are promoted to roles of leadership, they are often expected to abandon their valuable feminine characteristics. They are expected to lead like a man.

Making the conversation only about gender can cause us to miss the point. The spiritual leadership quiver must have a healthy dose of nurture, relational savvy, and intuition, regardless of the gender of the person occupying the position of leadership.

When we place someone in a position of authority, do we ever consider his or her ability to foster life, to intuitively receive direction from God, or to function from a place of relational connectedness? These feminine traits are significant in the functioning of the family known as "the church." Without them we effectively make our churches into single parent families. The young ones are always fathered and never mothered.

When we value these traits, we will look for them in males we hire. And we'll allow women in authority to express their true femininity as strength and not as a weakness.

8. WINESKINS INSTEAD OF PLANS

Finally a spiritual leader must learn the difference between a wineskin and a plan. Simply put, a wineskin is something that is designed to foster the presence of God. A plan is something that will work with or without God. Sometimes the difference between the two has more to do with our level of willingness to go on without God. It's one thing to say, "God, I'm not going another step unless you go with me." It's another to say, "God, this is where I'm going. I would prefer that you come along, but I'm going regardless."

Remember the story of the class I taught where as the class grew my own expectation of performance grew? In that same season, as I wrestled with performance the dynamic had been this: *I hear God early in the week; I teach what He said on Sunday.* He was always good to give me something to teach.

Until He wasn't.

One week, rather than giving me something to teach, I sensed that the Lord was asking me what I would do if He didn't give me anything. As is often the case His question seemed to dig into my heart and motives. I discovered my leaning was that I could make something up if He did not give me something,

I again sensed a question. "So you would do this without Me?" He seemed to ask. I sensed that the answer should be "no," but the clear inclination was that of course I would. People were showing up for a class; I should give them that.

I finally relented and said, somewhat honestly, "Of course, Lord, I would not teach if You did not give me something." You would think He would leave it at that, but somehow it seemed He wanted to test me. A few weeks later He gave me nothing. No matter how I tried, I seemed to get nothing from Him. And the test began. I began to rehearse my options. Make something up? Rehash an old lesson? The sifting in my soul grew.

And the week did not slow down. Finally Sunday arrived and I had nothing. I also had not decided whether I would go without Him or not. I finally relented and stood in front of a group who expected me to teach.

"I spent all week asking the Lord what to talk about and He gave me nothing," I said. "I can only assume that perhaps He gave one of you something."

Now most of you know that we had the best class ever that day. It just took me a while to see through my own journey that week that He was both testing me and showing me something.

Whether your goal is to help the struggling, train disciples or equip leaders—if the end goal is the restoration of God's Presence, then strategy becomes a secondary issue. In fact, strategy is only pertinent if it actually helps foster God's Presence.

Of course, life and practicality make real demands. At some point we must structure activities or outline a course of content. Leading people into encountering God does require some kind of plan. Whether it is a set list for a worship leader, or a curriculum for a teacher, a pro forma business plan for an administrator, or a get-out-of debt program for a young family—at some point a course must be set. Nevertheless, effective spiritual leaders must be able to say as Moses did, "If you do not go with me, I do not want to go."

The temptation to produce plans that work with or without God is a negative by-product of attracting people and the resulting pressure of their expectations. If two of us gather together, we may be content to wait to see what God is doing, but when you know 2,000 people are going to gather with an expectation that a specific lesson will be taught, or a certain gift will be manifested, or a certain number of songs will be sung (a few fast and a few slow, of course) the pressure to conform to those expectations soars. Crowds and expectations may make leaders more dependent on their natural strengths and skills than on God's active Presence.

In fact, any organization can at some point grow to a point where the organization itself becomes the purpose—replacing the vision that the organization was created to serve. This is an ever-present danger for growing organizations. And this pitfall isn't new.

Ezekiel 10 records what I think is one of the most chilling moments in the entire Old Testament narrative. I alluded to this a bit earlier, but allow me to employ a little poetic license to summarize the scenario.

The temple is organized. Highly organized. It has a multi-layered authority structure and a highly evolved division of labor. It has detailed processes refined over centuries—processes given by God Himself to facilitate His worship and His presence among His people.

Day after day, year after year, century after century—incense is being lit, ceremonial washings are being conducted and sacrifices are being offered. And God is present there. Then God gets up one morning and says to Himself, "I wonder what happens if I don't show up to church." God basically goes over and sits on the wall of the temple and watches the priests to see what they'll do if He's not there. Keep in mind that God's presence is supposedly the sole reason for everything they do.

And what happens? Jerusalem Temple, Inc. never misses a beat. The systems and the processes of temple worship go right on functioning. It seems no one even notices that the glorious presence of God has left the building. Incense, washing, sacrifice ... systems, processes, and policies all roll right along as before. How could this be?

Actually it's a common phenomenon. Gradually, stealthily, incrementally things get upside down. People create systems and processes, i.e. *organization*, to serve them in advancing their vision and purpose. But gradually we can find ourselves serving the systems instead of the systems serving us. The structure and processes became the thing rather than a means to the thing. When structures and processes become a god, the real God isn't likely to hang around for long.

But the truly terrifying thing about this is that we might not even notice! How chilling it is to contemplate that the Church could do everything it does every week—without God. This, I believe, is the danger of each generation of believers.

Something very similar happens in Christian organizations and ministry endeavors all the time. I would say that God's life-giving presence moves on from these enterprises for reasons both Heavenly and human. When men fail to discern that God has moved on, we are tempted to continue the practices out of habit, obligation, comfort or peer pressure.

This last factor, peer pressure, is particularly difficult to resist. It's possible to actually discern that something is wrong—to perceive that the Life of God is no longer animating and inhabiting our systems and processes—and yet be unwilling to face the disapproval and criticism that invariably comes from questioning deified organizational systems. Few rational humans want to be the only guy in the kingdom pointing out that the emperor is not wearing clothes.

Again, this is not to say that we have no need to make preparation, or develop strategies, structures and agendas. This is to say that our willingness to go on without God may just determine whether or not He goes with us.

While this section may sound like I am saying it is not a good idea to plan (especially to those who are averse to such labors), I am not saying that at all. What I am saying is that it is crucial to know the difference between wine (God's Presence) and the wineskin (our plans). God's presence and activity is the target. Our structures and processes should be built to support that, not to be a substitute for God's work.

As a matter of fact, the size of our wineskins may determine just how much wine shows up. When Jesus turned the water into wine in Cana, the amount of wine they ended up with was in direct, one-to-one correspondence to the number and size of pots the steward brought. Build your wineskins for however much wine you want. But stay alert to the difference between the wine and the wineskin.

I have become convinced over the years that God is more interested in people pursuing Him than He is in any one group being the ones who finally "get it right." Keep in mind that God's command not to make any graven image of Him was given, in part, because He defies definition in any single image or representation.

On man's side, I believe we may often be responsible for God's departure, whether character issues like pride or self-reliance directly begin to erode the integrity of a ministry, or these issues operate more subtly as we grow comfortable with our ability to "do this thing."

We know when to make a key change, when to emote a little more, when to pause for effect. We shift to rely on self, without even realizing it. When we drift into the common deception that the wineskin is the thing rather than the vessel that contains the thing, we enter the vast desert of dry, lifeless religion. We abandon our power to transform people and cultures.

Remember, mere human plans can be carried out and carried on without God's presence and animating power. But the nature of a true wineskin is that it will only function if God is present. Wineskins leave us beautifully, gloriously dependent upon God—a state that prideful human nature detests.

Finally, it's important to note that the bigger our wineskins, the greater our God-infused impact will be on this Earth. Like those clay water pots at the wedding in Cana, a greater capacity to contain vision and empowerment from Heaven means more of God's expanding, life-giving, freedom producing Presence being released on the Earth.

All of this prompts a question. How does a leader identify an organizational wineskin and, more vitally, how does he or she steward one? You won't be surprised to learn I have some thoughts about that. Onward.

CHAPTER 13

THE PRACTICES OF A SPIRITUAL LEADER

"Where the spirit does not work with the hand, there is no art."
—Leonardo da Vinci

"I must follow the people. Am I not their leader?"
—Benjamin Disraeli

All of Jerusalem was abuzz about the fledgling movement some were calling "The Way." The movement had burst onto the city's rich religious and cultural scene via a disruptive, impromptu preaching crusade on the Day of Pentecost—50 days after its founder had been executed following a high profile, controversial trial. (The body of that founder subsequently disappeared and hundreds claimed to have seen him alive and supernaturally glorified.)

The Way had begun as a structure-free amalgamation of about 120 individuals—eleven of whom had spent significant time with the founder over the preceding three years. Although three men—Peter, James and John—had all been a part of the founder's inner circle, there was no clear leader.

This seemed an improbable foundation for a wildly successful enterprise, and yet it was growing like crazy. In spite of social disapproval from Jerusalem's upper crust and even outright attempts at repression by the government, people were flocking to the movement by the thousands.

Eventually the rapid growth and sheer size of the enterprise began to create some challenges for the leaders of the new endeavor. One of the movement's core values was providing material support to widows and orphans. But complaints had begun to bubble up that this aid wasn't being distributed efficiently or fairly. After some prayer and discussion, a new level of organizational hierarchy was created—the office of *deacon*. Some criteria were established for selecting these new middle managers. And the deacons were charged with establishing some policies, protocols and processes that would facilitate the carrying out of the mission in accordance with the founder's values. This enabled the movement to continue sustaining the rapid growth that its abundant life and health were producing. Indeed, within 100 years, the movement had spread throughout the known world and was on a trajectory to change the course of human history.

First, organic life and health resulted in growth. Then, growth and size created a need. That need was for organization. Without some level of planning, management and organizing such growth would be unsustainable. Life generates the need for organization. (Of course, many leaders of the Way today have that precisely backwards. They seem to believe that superior organization will produce life. It can't.)

The movement's founder had once told his followers, "No one puts new wine into old wineskins. For the new wine would burst the wineskins, spilling the wine and ruining the skins. New wine must be stored in new wineskins." They didn't realize until much later that the Teacher wasn't really talking about wine.

What the disciples understood is that as new wine ferments, the "life" inside of it causes it to expand. A new wineskin has the capacity to stretch to accommodate this expansion. An old wineskin, on the other hand, has no stretch left in it. If you put new, life-filled, growing wine in one of these it will eventually rupture under the stress of the expansion.

Jesus used this illustration, along with one about patching an old garment with a piece of new, un-shrunken fabric, in the context of answering a question about why He didn't have His disciples do the same things in the same ways as the disciples of the Pharisees. The ways of the Pharisees had no life in them. Without life, there was no growth or expansion. Therefore their old processes, systems and structures seemed fine for them. Jesus was explaining that He was introducing a whole new Way. A living Way. And that the old systems, procedures and hierarchies would not be able to accommodate that life.

For the First Century Jerusalem church, life resulted in growth, which produced the need for organizational systems. As we discussed earlier what if another competing movement from across town observed this rapid growth with some envy? It's likely they would have said something like this to themselves, "Hey those guys over there are growing like crazy and they have this level of management they call deacon. That must be the secret to their growth. Let's adopt this deacon thing. It seems to work."

Something similar happens daily among churches in the Western world. We mistake effect for cause and emulate the wrong thing. We create structures and systems and end up desperately trying to breathe life into them, instead of connecting to the source of Life and then building structures and systems that are inspired and informed by that Life so it can be accommodated.

> **"THINGS LIKE VISION AND AUTHORITY ARE DISTRIBUTED THROUGH THE CHANNELS OF COMMUNICATION."**

Here's another thing we need to understand. Establishing a new organizational wineskin isn't a one-time thing. It is something that must be done at periodic points along the growth arc of a life-filled organization or movement. Ongoing life will necessitate the ongoing creation of new wineskins. So, it is worth taking time at this point of our journey to address some practical issues here in the development of organizations.

In practical reality, there is a bit of a balancing act as organizations begin to grow. On one hand, without structure, organizations become chaotic and unable to sustain growth and order. On the other hand, developing and maintaining structure requires a certain amount of time, energy, and spiritual wisdom. The balancing act is to invest in and structure the time and energy that is necessary to grow a healthy structure, without allowing the organization to become the central focus.

Like a political machine that requires staff, administration, processes, and hierarchy in order to perform its function, any organization must be developed and maintained. This takes time, people, money, and relational investment.

The specific purposes and goals of the organization must always be primary; and as discussed in the previous chapter, the ultimate goal of "seeking first the Kingdom" must be central to all of this development and maintenance. Building something that grows increasingly complex makes it increasingly difficult to maintain both original-mission-focus and a "seek first" approach. The system itself can begin to demand attention.

This balance should be monitored from multiple levels of an organization, as imbalance may show up more in one area than another.

It is also important to realize that just as a person can learn how to function to empower one kingdom more than another, so can an organization. Just as there are strongholds that come to exist in the development of our souls, strongholds can also grow in the development of an organization. Adding people to an organization adds relationships. Adding relationships provides one more way we can empower a spiritual realm. Here are some additional practical matters to consider:

Unity: Unity among people seems to be something toward which God commands His blessing. As we wrestle with the issues of vision, strategies and ways of handling people, organizations can either foster unity or foster division. The importance of prioritizing people and relationships isn't just a good leadership principle; it is the basis of organizational anointing.

Problem solving, conflict resolution, and team building all strengthen the unity of an organization and minimize potential organizational strongholds.

Family: Strategic partnerships and alignments are helpful for the transmission of ideas and data. Such relationships are entirely necessary as we develop concepts and strategies and must figure ways to share these kinds of exchanges.

It is crucial however to keep in mind that the mission or product of the church is not simply the transmission of ideas and data. The mission of the church is to receive, contain and broadcast the life of God. And God designed us in such a way that the institution of the family is the organization that produces life. Family relationships are different than partnerships; they are the necessary context to deliver this product we call *life*.

Family relationships have their genesis in a mutual bloodline. More so than doctrinal agreement or homogeneity, family relationships exist because of having the same Source. When we are related in that way, the nature of the relationship is not dependent on our ability to agree, but rather by the fact that we are already of one accord. Dress different? Talk differently? Probably, but we are still family because we have the same Father.

Family relationships, then, are also characterized primarily by love and connectedness. You know, the main thing that Jesus said would show others that we are His disciples? When we are related by ties that supersede intellectual or practical arrangements, we develop connections that can give away life.

John chapter 1 says that, *"In Him was Life, and that life was the light of all men"* (v. 4). The same substance exists in us. We do not pass it to others through instruction or organizational structure, we pass it on through love and connection.

While there are valuable things that we can pass on to others through a variety of means and types of relationships, we only pass on eternal things and we only pass on life through family relationships.

Communication: Effective communication is the lifeblood of unity. Any husband and wife can attest to the challenge of maintaining effective communication with only two people. Add numbers, add departments, add personalities and cultural diversity, and you will find you must do everything you can to foster effective communication.

Communication is the distribution of some pretty crucial elements for a spiritual system. Things like vision and authority are distributed through the channels of communication. Without such things, people perish, and power becomes unavailable. Effective communication is more than just good practice; it prevents the kingdom of darkness from playing its favorite game: Red Rover. You remember the game; two teams line up and hold hands. One team will call out, "Red Rover Red Rover, let Jason come over ..." and having chosen the smallest and least likely person to break through their line, the team calling out waits.

Jason has a different experience. Having been called out, he has something to prove. His assignment is to charge the line, find the weakest link, and break through, disconnecting one half of the team from the other.

The kingdom of darkness is constantly scanning for the weakest link. Disagreement, personality differences, judgments, unresolved conflicts, all of these create organizational strongholds.

Effective communication is more than just accurate transmission of data; it is the use of every available means to maintain shared meaning, shared vision and unity.

Clarity: *"Our God is not a God of confusion,"* Paul told the Saints at Corinth (1 Corinthians 14:33). Again, clarity is not simply a good communication strategy or value, it is an important aspect of God's nature. If this is true then confusion opens doors in our organizations for negative spiritual influence. It is difficult to be unified around what we do not understand.

Whether clarity is relative to purpose and vision, a new initiative, or how the organization is responding to a current challenge—this truth remains. The more things are clear, the less opportunity there is for a game of Red Rover to break out.

Employees/Subordinates: I had a conversation with a pastor who worked on my staff several years ago. A veteran of effective ministry for years, he declared his loyalty and submission to me and our mission. "Bob," he said, "I am here to fulfill your vision. What do you want me to do?"

"I disagree," I responded. "You are here to do what is in you to do"

"Respectfully," he began his next sentence, "I am here to serve you."

While I understood his heart and his message, I think it is crucial that we think through our entire conversation here. We have already established that the church is the corporate-ness of those of us who carry God's Presence in us through the new birth. When we develop structure and build ministry processes, we begin to think that we are here to do more than fulfill assignments. As mentioned earlier, though we may be employees, that is not our primary function.

Even in the selection of my employees, it is important that I take into account both assignment and identity. Another word for this is "calling." When I hire, I do the best I can to find someone with two qualifications.

First and utmost, I ask, "Is this the person that God has called here and now?" If so, my hiring of them now has eternal meaning and not just organizational helpfulness. That means that God has a purpose for them and us being together. Now, when we operate as team members, we are not just fulfilling job descriptions we are fulfilling destiny.

Second, I am trying to answer this question: "Will they have to become *someone* else in order to fulfill the assignment I am hiring them for?" Simply put, are they already "one of us?"

By this I want to be clear I am not referring to some "insider/outsider" mentality. What I mean is, if they are turned loose to be completely themselves, will they naturally build and oversee something very like or compatible with what the rest of the team is building? Is the vision already in them? If the answer to this is "no," we are already set up for tension. If the answer is "yes," then all I have to do is help them become themselves. If that happens they will produce far more than any other incentive could draw from them.

Discipline: Now the challenges come: substandard performance, poor compatibility and failures to cooperate on the parts of some team members. This is where the above ideas begin to be fleshed out. As best as we could answer the two vision questions above, we really begin to learn the definitive answers now as we work and live life together.

Whether in an organization or a family, issues of correction and discipline will arise. Issues of conflict and addressing these things from a hierarchical, oversight position are going to arise. These settings will test us and give us an opportunity as we have said, to empower one kingdom or another, and to lead people into either an encounter with God, or simply with human plans. *How* we handle these issues will determine which type of encounter our followers will have.

Discipline must be handled in ways that value people more than projects. Here, the value of clarity is vital. Disciplinary goals and issues must be spelled out clearly and specifically. Discipline must have both a path of restoration and a clear path of known consequences. Discipline must be redemptive and allow for an appeal process so that employees or followers are not shamed or left powerless under your authority.

Conflict Resolution: Perhaps no issue makes an organization more vulnerable than unresolved conflict. Unresolved conflict invariably finds a way to express itself—either overtly or covertly. Nevertheless, no issue is addressed or attended to less in the church than healthy handling of conflicts.

For a variety of reasons, we seem to steer away from handling conflicts, and so we certainly don't always develop habits that provide healthy resolution. In the healthy resolution of conflicts we must look at both structural/organizational matters, and then the strategy of conflict resolution itself. The two are directly related, and neither can exist without the other.

First (in sequence), we must recognize the structural/organizational issues in conflict resolution. So important is this that Jesus even devoted time to give guidance in this area (see Matthew 18 for example).

Organizationally, the most important aspect of handling conflict deals with knowing who to talk to, and who not to talk to. You can already see the problem here. At the very least, we have problems and we want people to pray for us—or at least that is what we tell ourselves. In an organization the only two types of people that you should talk to about your conflicts are the people with whom the conflict exists and the people who have the authority to do something about the conflicts.

But we seem to be regularly tempted to talk to the opposite kind of groups. We "want prayer" from those we are not in conflict with and prefer to talk to people who can do nothing about the issues.

As we think through Jesus' instructions in Matthew 18, let's apply this to organizations and conflict.

First, Jesus gives the simplest and most important instruction. If you have an issue with someone, go to *them*. The first level of conflict resolution would be to gather the people who are in conflict. No need for a petition, second opinion, or group of investors. Just go to the one with whom you are at odds. Many compounding issues could be avoided if this one simple step was practiced. Go to that person and see if you can work it out with them. If you are not satisfied with the result, Jesus says we should go back to them with witnesses. In an organization it is important not just to bring witnesses, but witnesses with the authority to resolve a dispute.

Ideally, this witness would be someone that has authority (organizational or familial) over both people involved. This allows them to offer more than just input; they can actually bring resolution. Appealing to the structures of authority allows all conflict to remain in the light and have the best possible chance for an easy resolution.

Given that the conversations happen with the right people, the next step is to be sure that conflict is addressed in right ways. Processes that move people toward real resolution include several important components.

The first component has to do with the spirit in which the conversation is approached. Assumptions about the participants and the goals of the conversation must be settled before the conversation even begins.

> "TO ASSUME THAT WE CAN LEAD AN ORGANIZATION TO PRODUCE SOMETHING THAT IS NOT BEING PRODUCED INTERNALLY LEAVES US CRIPPLED IN OUR MISSION."

This allows the process to begin in an atmosphere of trust. To assume that the other person is wrong or bad sets up an atmosphere of mistrust and creates a high likelihood of continued conflict. In contrast, assuming that the other person has a perspective that you do not, information that you do not, or may not have pertinent information that you do have, allows you to approach people assuming the best about them.

Next, the book of Proverbs (1:5; 18:13) tells us to seek first to hear and *then* to be heard. Listening is such an important part of all communication, and it is particularly important when dealing with emotionally charged exchanges.

The conflict should be defined in terms of issues to be understood and resolved, not as failures, accusations, character flaws, or weaknesses. Preferably, the issues should be defined in behavioral terms, not personal attacks. If the goal of the conversation can be agreed upon before it commences, the likelihood of positive outcomes increases.

Keep in mind, the point of all of this is that we, the Church, are God's chosen vehicle to restore His presence to the face of the Earth. If in our relationships we cannot foster God's Presence, we will struggle to do so corporately and we may disintegrate into a divided body.

If the primary evidence of being disciples of Jesus is that we love one another, it is crucial that we have skills and a plan to actually live this out. Merely avoiding conflict erodes love. Healthy conflict resolution strengthens and displays love.

Freedom: Jesus' mission was to set captives free. The mission of any spiritual leader must be the same. This is not an assignment exclusive to our congregation. We must assume this is an assignment for the people in our organization as well. If we try to lead people simply into the fulfillment of duties and the execution of events we may miss the greatest field for our mission, and minimize the greatest impact of our assignment.

Our working definition has been that freedom is when people can become the man or woman they are created and redeemed to be. Our oversight, our management, our implementation of strategy must have at its heart the target of the Kingdom, and the goal of setting our people free.

From the hiring process, through the fulfillment of mission, and at every juncture along the way, to assume that we can lead an organization to produce something that is not being produced internally leaves us crippled in our mission.

The idea of "the right person and the right seat on the bus" may be helpful for organizations and outcomes. The idea of processes designed to help people find their identity and purpose aligns us with the Kingdom of God, and achieves something far more eternal than just outcomes.

Lead your team in ways that allow them not to just to grow in skills. Help them to become themselves. When freedom is the process, freedom will always be the outcome.

CONCLUSION

You have arrived at the end of this work—but if I've done my job, not the end of your journey. On the contrary, my hope is that God has used this collection of thoughts and ideas to launch you on a fresh adventure. And that by examining and questioning some fundamental assumptions, you, a person called to point God's people toward the future, will go about that high calling in fresh ways. Or put another way, that you will think differently and therefore lead differently.

Before I send you on your way, allow me to remind you of the main waypoints we've visited on this journey so far. The challenge has been to think differently in these ways:

CHANGE THE RIGHT THING

We began in the first chapter admitting that, for a variety of reasons, the church has historically changed the wrong thing. That she has mis-treated because she has mis-diagnosed. And we learned that all change is not created equal, that there are actually *levels* of change.

CHANGE THE *HOW*, NOT THE *WHAT*

Jesus showed us a *Way*. When we are most authentically and organically expressing what Jesus wanted to leave behind on this Earth, we are truly "People of the Way." This truth must filter down to the way we affect change. More often than not, we don't have a *content* problem. We have a *process* problem.

UNDERSTAND THE TRUE MISSION OF JESUS

Jesus' mission was to rescue Original Design, not make bad people be good. He didn't come to fix our behavior (by moving us over to the "correct" branch of the Tree of the Knowledge of Good and Evil). He came to reconnect us to the Source (by restoring access to the Tree of Life). Jesus came to solve the problem of men and women being their own source.

KNOW THAT WHAT MAKES US "THE CHURCH" IS HAVING BEEN FATHERED BY THE RIGHT SOURCE

The Church is the corporate gathering of the People of the Way—people who contain the presence of God because they are born *of* Him and connected *to* Him.

THE CHURCH IS THE AGENCY IN THE WORLD THAT BRINGS GOD'S PRESENCE BACK TO THE PLANET

God's mission statement is to cover the Earth with His nature, and His strategy is you and me. It is the Church that will display God to a waiting, watching, aching world.

CHRISTIANITY IS A BELIEF SYSTEM BUILT UPON A WORLDVIEW THAT MOST PEOPLE NO LONGER HOLD AND FIND UTTERLY STRANGE

The dominant worldview here in the Western hemisphere is a blinding blend of rationalism and materialism. Holding that worldview actually makes it almost impossible to see or perceive the broader, wider, two-realm reality.

AUTHORITY IN ONE REALM DOESN'T NECESSARILY TRANSLATE INTO AUTHORITY IN ANOTHER

In the invisible realm spiritual authority is just as real and just as meaningful as is natural authority in the natural realm. Churches often promote to leadership people who are really good at Earth stuff. But being good at Earth stuff doesn't necessarily translate into being good at Heaven stuff. Spiritual authority functions in the connection between the natural and the supernatural realm.

AUTHORITY CAN BE COUNTERFEITED AND HIJACKED

Wherever you find real authority—natural or spiritual—you will invariably have people who try to attach themselves to the one who possesses that authority in order to gain influence. The "Jezebel spirit" seeks to hijack the legitimate leader's authority. Because man's soul empowers spiritual realities, bad authority produces dark results.

AUTHENTIC SPIRITUAL LEADERSHIP IS A JOURNEY

No, anyone who is an authentic leader in the Kingdom—wielding both natural and spiritual authority—didn't get to that place in a day. It was a journey. Some common, predictable milestones characterize this process. One of the most significant of these is a soul-searing encounter with rejection.

AUTHENTIC SPIRITUAL LEADERS HOLD KEY VALUES

A spiritual leader is guided by some specific ways of seeing, which produces a distinct set of emphases. These include a focus on "the Kingdom," a focus on hearing the voice of God, and a commitment to making disciples rather than dependents.

EFFECTIVE SPIRITUAL LEADERS ENGAGE IN CERTAIN PRACTICES

Truly effective leaders commonly do some key, common things. They pursue life and health rather than growth—knowing that growth will be a natural result. They create new organizational "wineskins" in response to that growth. They cultivate unity, operate like family, facilitate communication, promote freedom, and much more.

MATURE SPIRITUAL LEADERS PURSUE COMMON TARGETS

The Kingdom model of leadership requires pursuing some specific ends and outcomes. These include leading people to encounter God for themselves, teaching them to hear God for themselves, and helping them discover their true *identity* in God.

There you have it. My humble offering of a new model for raising up and equipping authentic people of the Way. A challenging call to abandon lemming leadership. That is, to stop thinking that we're leading effectively simply because people are following us. A challenge to stop talking *about* The Game, and instead lead by playing it fervently, joyously, recklessly well.

Want to play?

THINK DIFFER ENTLY LIVE DIFFER ENTLY

Keys to a life of freedom

So you're new to the think differently conversation are you? I hope by the time you have arrived here, you have enjoyed a journey of pushing hard at paradigms, and dismantling barriers in your mind. If you're wondering about the first book I mentioned, I wanted to give you a chance to at least glance at it and see if it might have the same effect on your soul.

Beginning on the next page is a taste of the story that has launched thousands on their own personal journey to a new life. This story, in it's entirety is Chapter One and Chapter Six of *Think Differently Live Differently*. It's my story. And it's your story. And it's the story of a loving father who has lost his son.

As a result it will be a familiar story, and this is by design. Find yourself in the next few pages, it shouldn't be hard to do. What would be more important is if somehow as you read, you also allow yourself to be found.

CHAPTER 1

THE PARABLE OF THE ACROBAT

"... you know something. What you know you can't explain, but you feel it. You've felt it your entire life, that there's something wrong with the world. You don't know what it is, but it's there, like a splinter in your mind, driving you mad."
— Morpheus, The Matrix

"We were meant to live for so much more, have we lost ourselves ..."
— Switchfoot, Meant to Live

This was more than she could bear. Life in a traveling troupe had never been particularly easy, but this was a tragedy greater than her heart could stand. Her only child had vanished in one horrible moment.

The loss was not hers alone. This baby boy—although the smallest member of this troupe of world-class acrobats—embodied its greatest hopes for the future. So, while his mother sobbed, the rest of the group continued their desperate search. It was fruitless. Despite their strength, skill and passionate determination, they could not find him.

Prior to this day, only excitement and expectation had animated conversations about her son. Today, a hushed fear infused every word. Her child was lost in the middle of a foreign wilderness; and she was inconsolable.

Dreadful possibilities tormented her thoughts so she fled to the refuge of happier memories. She replayed that joyful day, several months ago, when her son was born.

She had been the rising star among the women of the troupe. All who watched her recognized athletic gifts. No other female acrobat could match her strength, agility and balance. When it was her turn to perform, even her talented peers were mesmerized by her unique abilities. Even so, she carried herself with a gracious humility.

They also held the man she married in high regard. He was the only other acrobat who performed with equal strength and skill. The entire troupe, already known for near superhuman feats, recognized these two as the greatest athletes they had ever seen. The couple was also well-matched as soulmates. Instead of falling prey to inflated egos, they both possessed a gentleness of spirit and depth of character. They were dearly loved and admired, and they were the heart and soul of their community.

When the celebrated couple announced the joyful news that they were expecting a baby, there was a great deal of excited speculation among their friends about the promising future of their child. Needless to say, everyone had high expectations for the offspring of such gifted parents. When the mother-to-be would comment on the movement of the baby inside her womb, it was met with humorous replies that, no doubt, the child was already perfecting his skills before making his debut. Each person carried in their own imagination the heights he would reach and the amazing feats he would perform.

> **"HE ALREADY POSSESSED THE GENETIC BLUEPRINT FOR EVERY INNATE DRIVE AND ABILITY CARRIED BY HIS TWO PARENTS. SURELY, THE HOPE FOR THEIR FUTURE WAS EMBODIED IN THIS NEW LITTLE CREATION."**

He already possessed the genetic blueprint for every innate drive and ability carried by his two parents. Surely, the hope for their future was embodied in this new little creation.

On the day of his birth, the entire troupe gathered outside in nervous, giddy anticipation, awaiting the first audible evidence of the baby's appearance. Before he had even arrived, they all knew that he was destined to be a great acrobat. Oh what a joyous day that had been. But then came that other day . . .

That day the unthinkable happened. Reaching into the back of the wagon to awaken her infant, she found an empty pallet. Everything else was intact, but the baby boy was nowhere to be found. Somewhere along the way he had fallen! Though they spent the day backtracking and searching for clues, the heavily traveled trails held no evidence of the tragedy. As the daylight faded, so did their hopes of ever recovering the child of promise. The somber whispers of the troupe and the sobs of his mother as she clutched the empty blankets left behind were the only evidence that the infant had even been among them. He was gone.

RESCUED—OR WAS HE?

It had to be divine intervention that protected the child from the elements and the wild animals that day. Sadly, his parents did not have the comfort of this knowledge. They could not have known that hours earlier that day, another man and wife made their way down the same trail. Walking back to their modest farm, they heard an odd sound in the brush, so they turned aside to see what it might be.

Parting the grass which grew tall beside the trail, the woman looked down. Outwardly, she was shocked, but inside, a strange hope awakened as she recognized that what they had heard was a little baby, crying there in the ditch by the road.

She had agonized over her barrenness. Her dreams of motherhood had long ago expired. It had been years since she had allowed herself the luxury of yearning for a child to call their own. Her husband, a hard man, had long ago stopped accommodating her sadness. So, she bore it with quiet stoicism.

But the discovery sent those emotions cascading through her again. What was a baby doing here? The only people nearby were the neighboring farmers, tucked into the privacy of their homesteads. None of them would have brought such a young child out on this road. What should they do? Finding the child's parents might prove impossible, and if they did find them, what if they had abandoned him on purpose? If they didn't find them, what could they do? They were ill-prepared to raise a child, but they couldn't just leave him here!

She glanced at her husband, fearful of the look she might see on his face. He showed no outward reaction, but his eyes were locked on the infant. His lack of expression was familiar. The only emotion she had seen from him in recent years was anger. Hard times had made him a hard man. Decent, but hard—and increasingly introverted, showing little in the way of warmth or affection.

Thus she suspected that his comfort level in raising a child would be even lower than hers.

After a terse exchange, they agreed to take the child home and do all they could to find his parents or a suitable home for him. Fear gripped her. Despite her desire to be a mother, she knew she lacked the knowledge and experience to raise a child and that they had very little to offer this one. She suspected this chance discovery would utterly change their lives. But it was impossible for her to know all that lay ahead.

She carried the infant home with great trepidation. Doing the best she could, she worked on the immediate task of feeding the child and finding appropriate bedding for one so small. Each cough and gurgle from the infant solicited a growing motherly affection within her, but also provoked more worry.

They knew very little about the baby they had rescued, but neither of them could have dreamed that they were holding the child of perhaps the two greatest acrobats in the world. Not only did he prove to be quite healthy, but from the very start he had a burning desire to defy gravity and to push the edge of physical limitations. He was made for more than crawling and walking—he wanted to fly.

He was born to live in a world he knew nothing about. He was born for a life of transcendence.

*****

This is where the story begins. As the parable unfolds it gives us a new lens through which we can view the Gospel, but it also launches us on the journey. Specifically, it launches us on the journey where, in discovering who we are, we begin to actually become who we are.

This is the journey of freedom. And this is the journey of Think Differently Live Differently. This is the journey where the real you inside is set free from the you that you have become.

Let the young acrobat help you learn to again defy gravity. Let him help you find the path where the Father who has found you, walks you into a life of deep freedom and transformation. Let him help you think differently about you and the God who made you.

Think Differently Live Differently: Keys to a Life of Freedom can be found at bobhamp.com, Amazon, or your local bookstore. Dive in.